9780317549867

A DIRECTORY OF
ANTIQUE
FURNITURE

A DIRECTORY OF ANTIQUE FURNITURE

F. LEWIS HINCKLEY

THE AUTHENTIC CLASSIFICATION OF
European and American Designs
FOR PROFESSIONALS & CONNOISSEURS

BONANZA BOOKS · NEW YORK

TABLE OF CONTENTS

PREFACE	VII
INTERRELATION OF FURNITURE DESIGNS	IX
THE SPREAD OF FRENCH AND ENGLISH DESIGN INFLUENCES	
GERMANY	XI
LIEGE AND AIX LA CHAPELLE	XV
AUSTRIA	XV
DENMARK	XVI
DANISH WEST INDIES	XVIII
BERMUDA	XIX
SWEDEN	XIX
NORWAY	XX
RUSSIA	XXI
HOLLAND	XXII
DUTCH COLONIES	XXIV
CHINA AND THE PHILIPPINES	XXV
IRELAND	XXVI
STRUCTURAL METHODS AND MATERIALS	XXIX
ILLUSTRATIONS	
PART I Furniture Related to the French School (Plates 1-159)	1
PART II Furniture Related to the English School (Plates 160-398)	62
PART III French Furniture, Based on Paris Designs (Plates 399-496)	133
PART IV English Furniture, Based on London Designs (Plates 497-676)	162
PART V Irish Furniture, Based on English and Continental Designs (Plates 677-878)	221
PART VI American Furniture, Based on English and Irish Designs (Plates 879-1103)	282

(C)

Copyright, 1953, by F. Lewis Hinckley • Library of Congress Catalog Card Number: 52-10776 • Printed in the United States of America

Preface

AUTHENTICITY is the primary concern of the prospective as well as the confirmed collector of antique furniture. Usually he looks for originality (authenticity) in the condition of pieces under consideration. Less frequently is he concerned with origin according to the manufacturing centers where furniture designs of the various style periods were evolved, and those in which such designs were followed after they had been developed and had gained favor elsewhere. However, origin should be an important concern of students and collectors, particularly those interested in American designs, for the styles which were evolved on the Continent, in England and in Ireland, before finally appearing here, will be more readily understood in their ultimate renditions if all earlier phases of their evolution are known.

Fifteen years in the field of antique furniture, prior to World War II, aroused my interest in alien designs which were exhibited and accepted as indigenous to England, France and America. I then undertook investigations in this country and abroad to determine the sources of these designs. When it was possible to resume this study, I visited many more of the European furniture centers to acquire a first-hand knowledge in details of design and construction. Professional requirements in appraising for private collectors, and authenticating furniture for public sale, made possible an even broader view of furniture design, extending to all parts of the world. I also derived information from among a wide acquaintance of those professionally engaged in buying and selling antiques.

Appreciation of time given in these interests is due Messrs. D. H. Lavezzo, his sons Daniel and John, Gaston Bensimon, Mitchel Samuels, Nicholas De Koenigsburg, A. Wittekind, S. Berges, M. Ullman, Joe Kindig, I. Sack, Benjamin Ginsburg, Bernard Levy and I. Winick. Mr. Jack Treleaven has been particularly helpful in regard to Irish chairs and tables, and Mr. J. J. Wolff, concerning Irish mirrors. Mrs. Anne Goldsmith has graciously read, and offered valuable advice on, notes from which the present manuscript is derived. Mrs. Margot Brockhues and Mr. Eric Marquis have supplied many translations of foreign texts.

In Europe, Th. H. Lunsingh Scheurleer, Esq., of the Rijksmuseum, Amsterdam, Andre Leth, Esq., of Det Danske Kunstindustri Museum, Copenhagen, and Marshall Lagerquist, Esq., of the Nordiska Museet, Stockholm, were equally generous with their time, given to discussing furniture of their respective countries. I owe thanks to the many owners and curators of public and private collections that I visited in Europe, especially where examination of furniture was made possible by the gracious removal of obstacles and coverings, as in the Museum fur Kunst und Gewerbe, Hamburg, and at the Six collection in Amsterdam.

Messrs. Taylor and Dull, leading photographers of furniture and objects of art in this country, are responsible for the fine work in many of the illustrations appearing in this book. They have displayed their usual outstanding camera skills, and have succeeded in featuring all details of importance to the present subject.

While photography has added to studies of all the arts, published illustrations of various works, accompanied by incorrect designations, have resulted in long existent misconceptions of design. This is particularly true in regard to furniture. Illustrations of antique furniture are of great value when studied in conjunction with the handling of the actual pieces. When immediate access to a wide variety of examples is not possible, illustrations may then serve to a considerable extent in the study of furniture designs. Details, in addition to general forms, should be memorized. When such features of design are mentally retained, they will prove to be of real importance in correctly determining both genuine examples, and those which may be genuine as far as age is concerned, but which are incorrectly labeled as to provenance. Errors in this direction, which are not recognized, can result only in misunderstanding of design and further mistakes in classification.

Certain collections of French, English or American furniture contain pieces that originated else-

VII

where. Similarity of design, woods and mounts, and the blending influence of time have permitted many of these pieces to merge with a majority of correctly attributed examples. Like errors may be found where such foreign pieces appear in illustrated form, intermixed with correctly classified pieces, particularly where illustrations do not appear in an orderly sequence.

The ability to recognize and properly to classify illustrated or exhibited specimens will be aided by a knowledge of the interrelated designs which developed throughout various sections of the world, and also through some understanding of the vast commerce which resulted in delocalizing so many examples. These phenomena are featured here as especially significant to the study of antique furniture. The comparison of related examples with those representing a major school from which they were derived, or which they may parallel in some respects, is essential to amplify differences and similarities in such designs. I have selected the illustrations of Continental, English, Irish and American furniture with a view toward making these comparisons as clear as possible.

Interrelation of Furniture Designs

DURING recent decades collectors, more than ever before, have placed emphasis on quality, interest, rarity and beauty in the purchase of antique furniture. Despite the desire to own examples which are authentic, and whose value will increase, collectors have given little attention to certain essential knowledge pertaining to design. I refer to originality based on the various centers in which fine furniture was formerly produced, rather than "originality" as it is so widely used today, describing authenticity in the original material condition of an object.

The great schools of furniture design which arose in Europe following the Dark Ages received their stimuli not only from local talent but from designers and craftsmen attracted from adjoining or even distant areas. Skills thus cultivated and fostered were by no means stationary. Craftsmen not only visited the large centers to improve their techniques, but they later carried their newly acquired skills to their own or other countries. Leading craftsmen of these centers also visited or established themselves elsewhere. Consequently, designs and tectonic methods were intermingled and widely spread. Some maintained continuity with the principles of a particular school, others merged with the designs of various areas. Thus, when the French and English schools of design rose to preeminence during the eighteenth century, and were followed throughout Europe and America, designs or elements thereof which originated in England and France were copied elsewhere in Europe and in America, as well as in various colonies.

In studying and comparing the furniture of the countries which were themselves centers of influence, and the furniture of other areas which produced work more or less taken from, or parelleling, these centers, complete attention should be accorded to all the smallest details of design. In such a study a number of examples, with no particular appeal because of certain peculiarities in their designs, may be passed over without due consideration. However, these will often contain valuable clues to help assign other examples to the areas where such design peculiarities were permitted, or even favored.

All too frequently foreign elements are disregarded. Yet anyone who fails to take such elements into consideration shows such a lack of understanding and discernment as to eliminate him as an authority. To possess authoritative knowledge concerning the antique furniture of any country, one must also be equally informed about related designs produced in all other countries or areas reached by similar design influences.

The numerous pieces of furniture which today are attributed to France, England and America far exceed the possible output of the craftsmen of these countries. Records of the settlement of immigrant craftsmen do not indicate enough production to account for the difference. Natively executed work is sometimes verified through the presence of indigenous materials. However, definite structural determination, sometimes found in the secondary woods of American pieces, particularly poplar, is seldom as positive in Europe, where native species of timber were widely grown and distributed.

Design, therefore, becomes a principal factor in deciding the geographic origin of furniture, with exposed structural features included as pertinent elements, often of greater importance than those concealed. Though pedigrees are also to be considered, flaws in such documentation are frequent, so that they should be weighed carefully.

Foreign furniture was seldom copied exactly, although this did occur. Instead there were adaptations, often rather free, to suit the preferences of a particular craftsman or shop owner, to conform with local tastes, or to make use of such materials as were readily available. Drawings and details made by migratory workers were sometimes used, as well as those of specializing designers. Wealthy patrons, too, sent native architects to study at the principal art centers so that they would be better equipped to design appropriate interiors and furnishings for their benefactors. As commerce increased, designs might be more accurately translated in areas separated by sea, than by land, because of the greater obstacles of overland travel.

When furniture design became increasingly influenced by both French and English styles, still greater interrelationship resulted. Pieces were eventually developed which might well be described by hyphenated phrases, such as "Louis XV-Chippendale" or "Directoire-Sheraton" designs.

Various minor effects of interrelation will become apparent when the spread of design influence is discussed. Principal factors which resulted in the interrelation of designs may be summarized as follows:

When the work of designers or craftsmen of different areas—neighboring or distant—during any particular period contains a few basic elements in common, some generally similar patterns will be produced, no matter how divergent the majority of native designs may be.

When these common basic elements are improved or elaborated on from an outside center of influence, some parallel designs are bound to be produced, not only in the affected area and the center, but also in any other area influenced by the center.

When any area is motivated by the designs of two independent centers of influence at the same time, resulting productions may approximate those of either or both of these centers, or those of other areas influenced by the two centers.

If these rules are considered in studying the evolution of furniture designs, prior to the sixteenth century, during the Renaissance and throughout the later decorative periods when travel and commerce increased more rapidly, it will be found that relationships progressed accordingly.

Recognition of these relationships, particularly in reference to furniture following the French and English styles, is essential today because of widespread delocalization. This resulted from demands of traders and collectors during the past one hundred and twenty years, and also from deliveries to foreign shores at the time that the pieces were originally produced.

Furniture supplied but a small part of commercial ventures during the sixteenth and seventeenth centuries. Its widespread distribution is accounted for in part by emigrations, such as that of William Penn's colonists from England, Ireland and Wales, who arrived here with their own furniture, tools, implements, and even *houses in frames,* and a *mill ready framed.*

During the eighteenth century there was far greater movement of furniture in Europe. Pieces from France, Italy, Germany, Holland, Sweden, Denmark, England and Ireland were shipped to both neighboring and distant areas. Toward the end of this century American furniture was dispatched to the West Indies, South America, and occasionally to Northern Europe. Previously America had been the recipient of furniture from England, Ireland, Sweden, Denmark, North Germany, Holland and France.

Further delocalizing effects followed. During the first half of the nineteenth century collecting of *curious and ancient furniture, both in foreign countries and in England,* was inaugurated by London tradesmen, who were then recorded as possessing *extensive collections of Elizabethan and Dutch furniture* to remake in the taste of the time. Later in the century private collections of French and Italian Renaissance furniture were formed, and English tastes veered toward eighteenth century examples from France.

English interest in collecting native specimens of antique furniture later increased. To supply this demand it became necessary to draw upon two *substitute* sources of supply: Ireland and North Germany. Deliveries of examples from the latter country, which might pass as English, were made through North Sea and Baltic ports to England and Scotland. This trade was carried on extensively from 1890 to 1920, at which time central and southern German states were replenishing stocks removed from Hamburg. Trade with Ireland continued to flourish until more recent years. Irish examples which had been finely designed and executed were generally regarded as having originated in England. Only lesser pieces were attributed to Irish hands. Dublin also provided a principal source of supply for mantels, especially those associated with the name of Bossi, an Italian artisan who worked in this locale and for Robert Adam in England.

Modern appreciation of antique French furniture has resulted in traders' visits to all of the European countries to which such examples had been sent in the past. Many pieces were thus placed in circulation again, accompanied by a still greater number of foreign examples which might pass, with occasional alterations, as French in design and execution.

With the development of American interest in collecting English furniture, Irish and Continental examples began to find their way into shipments destined for this country. In some instances, eighteenth century pieces which had originated in the Baltic areas, and had been sent as far east as Poland, have come to light in America, being acquired here as products of Colonial craftsmanship.

Knowledge of this type of delocalization and the recognition of relationships existing between designs produced throughout the Occident are both highly pertinent to the study of antique furniture. They are often important factors in determining correct origins. Unfortunately, there are experts who fail to consider these factors, with the result that incorrectly identified pieces can be found in some of the finest public and private collections.

The Spread of English and French Design Influences

GERMANY

COLLECTORS, who exhibit certain examples of furniture as French, English or American, frequently lower their opinions of the merit of such pieces on learning that they actually originated in Germany. Other German designs are accepted as Dutch, Flemish, French Provincial, Iberian or Italian. Collectors as a whole, not to mention institutions exhibiting antique furniture, are unaware of the different schools which were followed, and the many designs evolved throughout the independent German states.

If all works of art were to be assessed according to quality of design and craftsmanship, the finest German furniture would be ranked with important French and English specimens. While many examples do receive such regard in France, the situation is different in England and America. When an important specimen in an English collection is proven to be of German origin, a lawsuit may result because of the drastic reduction in market value.

The pecuniary appreciation of English furniture exceeds that of Continental furniture produced in more or less related patterns. In instances when Continental examples have been sold for about the same prices as somewhat similar English productions, it has been held that the purchasers received less than full value. Therefore, an exceptionally fine lacquered or veneered piece, far exceeding English costs and skills in manufacture, but executed in Saxony or Brandenburg, is not valued as highly today as a supposedly comparable English specimen. Nobody can deny the existence of quality and artistic merit in such German examples. Since they have been deemed worthy of association with other fine pieces of English origin, their equal or greater value may eventually be recognized.

German authorities readily acknowledge indebtedness to French and English designs. However, they take great pride in their own contributions, which may be seen in more typically native productions. In major German towns statutes governing the service of furniture apprentices and journeymen were as rigidly enforced as those effective in France and England. Apprentice training consisted of several years in a master's shop, followed by over a decade as a journeyman. Many journeymen worked in France, Italy and England. To qualify as a master it was necessary to produce a *piéce de maîtrice,* as in Paris, designed and made by the applicant alone.

Master cabinetmakers often cast and finished their own decorative appliqués, modeled after those of France and England, sometimes with added elements of native design. Such resourcefulness saved Dresden ateliers considerable sums which might otherwise have gone to France and England. Sculptors and painters also collaborated with cabinetmakers, supplying carved, painted and gilded effects, as had been done in Italy. Various influences, such as geography, temperament, political conditions and the work of neighboring craftsmen, resulted in a great diversity of talents and matériel in the design and construction of fine furniture.

In the southern German states craftsmen, influenced by the bravura of the Italians, introduced their spirited embellishments in examples which were further inspired by the French. Talent in the western and central states was largely influenced by France and The Netherlands. In northern sections stimuli came from Holland, France and England, while some interchange of ideas occurred between North German and Scandinavian areas.

The vitality of acquired ideas, added to the best native skills, resulted in a continuous development of techniques in leading manufacturing centers, which were later spread to many smaller towns. During the seventeenth century a number of craftsmen had already surpassed the accomplishments of French and English cabinetmakers, although, in general, refined designs and accomplished working methods were developed after the middle of the eighteenth century. At this time, while French craftsmen were merely repeating established designs, the more sophisticated of the German variations displayed a greater originality. Similarly, popular native themes frequently added interest to repeated English designs.

In the castles and smaller homes of the noble and wealthy families great sums were lavished on architecural features and specially made furniture. The architect, Joseph Effner, mentor of François Cuvilliés, was responsible for important commissions of this type in Bavaria, notably in Munich, which was one of the finest and handsomest towns in Europe during the early eighteenth century. François Cuvilliés was taken into the service of the elector of Bavaria, sent to Paris to study under the masters there, and became one of the leading interpreters of the Rococo style, along with his countrymen, the Slotz brothers, and the Italian, Meissonnier.

Johann Michael Hoppenhaupt and F. X. Haberman were the principal exponents of the native Rococo school affecting designs to the north. Renditions of their projects in Brandenburg often appear as close approximations of French creations in furniture and interiors, executed with imagination and with considerable delicacy and grace.

Furniture skills existent in Berlin and Potsdam during the middle of the eighteenth century, at such workshops as were maintained by the Spindlers and Melchior Kambly, could well rival those of Paris. While favored contours often present divergencies from the more usual French outlines, they appear as welcome contrasts, and possess decided vigor and interest, accompanied by highly skilled work in marquetry or lacquer decoration, and rhyming appliqués of gilded bronze.

During his reign, King Frederick William built numerous fine houses for the inhabitants of Potsdam. His son, Frederick the Great, contributed still further to the embellishment of this town after ascending the throne in 1740. Various apartments in the Potsdam palace and at Sanssouci, which were then furnished, have been widely illustrated and amply portray the prevailing mode. In adjoining Berlin, the larger and more ancient capital city, Frederick II was even more liberal in his rebuilding projects. It was here that French and English influences were shared in designs chosen from among those offered by Hepplewhite, and by publications of less authoritative nature.

Of the many German *ébénistes* who were accepted masters in Paris during the reign of Louis XV, and particularly in that of Louis XVI, Oeben, Riesener, Beneman and Schwerdfergei designed and worked with full acceptance of the Gallic spirit. A considerable number of their countrymen, however, retained native characteristics. These are apparent in the work of Wolff, Schlichtig, Rubestock, Grenevich, Joseph (Joseph Baumhauer) and Shiller. It is apparent that German cabinetmakers, and craftsmen who specialized in supplying marquetry, were more assured of success in Paris than were chair-makers.

Adam Weisweiller is also representative of the German-trained craftsman who executed refined designs distinguished by lack of heaviness and floridity. He is acknowledged as one of the most brilliant *ébénistes* of his time. Weisweiller is reputed to have been born in the town of Neuwied, adjoining Coblentz, and to have received his technical training in the atelier of David Roentgen.

David Roentgen (1743-1807) came to be known as *le plus célèbre ébéniste de l'Europe* after taking over the establishment which had been founded by his father in Neuwied. This event took place in 1772, and marks a change from the more strongly characteristic German designs of the elder Roentgen. David traveled widely in Europe, accompanied by vans containing selected examples of Neuwied productions. It has been said that on a first trip to St. Petersburg he secured the interest of Catherine the Great through his resourcefulness in arranging, overnight, for a clock in a *secretaire* to commemorate a Russian naval victory that had just occurred at Tschesmé. (The date of this victory is given by Russian historians as occurring in 1770, so that the story must be discounted; and David's popularity with Catherine II was subject to her vagaries. However, between 1783 and 1791 he visited St. Petersburg frequently, supplying the Empress with numerous examples of work turned out at Neuwied.) Many of Roentgen's pieces were made expressly for such commercial enterprises, and therefore could be dismantled so that they would take up the least possible van space (see Fig. 114).

A first visit to Paris in 1774 proved so successful that subsequently David Roentgen maintained a warehouse there. His furniture, however, was always produced in Neuwied. It is claimed that he also opened warehouses in Berlin and Vienna. He was not a member of the Paris *ébénistes* corporation until 1780, and as a foreigner was free of the rule governing the stamping of furniture with an identifying *pontil* mark. In some instances, however, the important and finely executed productions of the Neuwied factory are distinguished by the initials, "D.D.," or other identification in marks or inlays.

David Roentgen apparently owed his business success in part to his exceptionally handsome appearance and ingratiating manner. Of equal significance were the elaborate fittings and mechanical devices built into his furniture, and the skills of his craftsmen in carrying out the techniques favored in Neuwied, as in the marquetry work of Chrétien Krause and Michael Rummer, and the mechanical ability of Johann Roetig. Assistance to other cabinet shops in North Germany, Paris and Copenhagen, was rendered by David, his technicians and his brother, George Roentgen. It is claimed that Chippendale's *Director* was used by Abraham Roentgen, father of David, after his return from working in Galway, Ireland, previous to 1750. John Okely, an English youth, was apprenticed to the elder Roentgen, while in turn he sent one of his own craftsmen to London for training.

Investigations attempting to determine the origin of the New England blockfront designs have long ignored the typically native designs produced in southern and central German states through the second quarter of the eighteenth century, and later in states as far north as Mecklenburg and Holstein (see Fig. 252). Once these German and Danish blocked forms were adopted here, craftsmen of different nationalities collaborated in their production. This is indicated by hints of English, Irish or Dutch structural techniques. However, German origin is further substantiated by the frequent appearance of twin moldings on the upper edges of pine or poplar drawer sides, a definite Germanic detail.

Marked English influence, which appeared in these states during the middle of the century, was centered in Hanover and the numerous adjoining duchies, principalities and free cities, in Mecklenburg, Pomerania and the vicinity of Danzig. This influence appeared in furniture approximating Early Georgian designs, which were followed until 1770 or later. In Brunswick, however, the furniture brought over by the royal English bride of Prince Karl Wilhelm Ferdinand, in 1764, is said to have caused considerable attention and admiration, and to have been regarded as the first of such examples seen there.

More distinct English influence was felt after 1770, and in a wider variety of forms. This is noticeable in designs copying the true Chippendale style, following the general adoption of straight legs. From this time on English designs were copied in the North, in Brandenburg, Anhalt, Weimar and Saxony. In the vicinity of Berlin, rooms were furnished in the style of Sir William Chamber's *chinoiserie* creations, and in the mode developed by Robert Adam, with perhaps the closest approximations in mirror frames and balancing wall treatments. Wedgwood plaquettes were supplied in copies made at Cassel. Angelica Kauffman, a favorite artist of Robert Adam, not only portrayed German and Danish nobility, but her classic figural studies were lent to the prevailing *décor*.

Chippendale and Adam styles were followed in chairs and settees, occasional tables, tables with fret galleries, chests of drawers, cabinets and secretaries. The evolution of native designs, influenced by the same Italian and French sources that were drawn upon in England, produced many "Louis XVI-Adam" effects, and some of those which approached Chippendale forms.

The Berlin Academy of Art, in 1777, on determining which of the *ébénistes* working there, according to the native, French and English schools, might be qualified for academic honors, selected as suitable only those who followed the English school.

Designs from Hepplewhite's *Guide* were particularly favored in Germany as a source of patterns for backs of seat furniture. These were sometimes selected from plates which had greater appeal to local tastes than to those of English chair-makers or their patrons. Sheraton's remarks concerning Continental interest in English furniture designs no doubt referred specifically to the use of English designs in Germany and in Denmark. There was even greater evidence of this interest when a group of Sheraton's own designs were published at Leipzig in 1794.

The skills which German craftsmen displayed in carrying out Georgian designs were recognized by George Smith in *The Cabinet-Maker and Upholster's Guide,* with its introducted dated in 1826. After eulogizing the ability of the English craftsman, and disparaging that of the French *ébéniste* in regard to construction and design, his second paragraph under *Cabinet Furniture* is devoted to praise of German cabinetmakers working in England before, and during, his time. "In this place we must not omit to mention another race of artizans: viz. the Germans, as being ingenious in almost every branch of mechanical art placed under their hands: they possess the grand essential toward producing good work, viz. that of patience, if they are not altogether so quick and fanciful as the French on that which relates to design. Some years back many of these artizans worked in several of our cabinet manufactures, but have since emigrated almost all of them into the musical establishments of Messrs. Broadwoods, Muzio Clementi, Stodart and others."

English designs were introduced even more widely in local periodicals, such as the *Magazin für Freunde des guten Geschmackes,* the *Journal für Manufaktur-Fabriken* and the *Journal des Luxus und der Moden.* In addition, craftsmen had access to imported English furniture, which was displayed and sold in local warerooms, and ordered directly from London by the nobility and more affluent citizenry.

A new method of decorating furniture and smaller objects, in lacquer, had been discovered in 1758 by Johann-Heinrich Stobwasser (1740-1829), who afterwards founded a successful manufactory at Brunswick, and in 1772 opened a branch in Berlin. He produced furniture, coffrets, snuff boxes and other small objects in wood and papier-mâché, designed after both the native and English tastes. These were decorated in his lacquer finish and painted by the finest artists available. In executing a royal order to copy a table which had been ordered from London, he succeeded so well that his work was considered superior to the original.

Mirror frames of the more formal carved and gilded designs were, in general, elaborately rendered throughout Germany up until the Classic period. During the Rococo era gilding was sometimes replaced by a grained finish, simulating mahogany or walnut. Outside influences stemmed from Italy and France. While English influence was present during the Classic period, this did not affect these formal designs to any great degree, although a few pieces have been accepted as true Adam and Hepplewhite specimens. Original makers' labels were affixed to some mirror backs during the Classic period, but these have generally been removed.

Mirror frames veneered in walnut and mahogany, with gilded wood or gesso ornament, were produced in North Germany, and in neighboring Danish areas, where Altona, a principal center in this production, adjoined Hamburg. Designs in these two areas were thus closely related, and were influenced by similar external motivations.

It is apparent that shipping activities were in part responsible for various relationships in "Queen Anne" and "Georgian" types of frames, which were often produced later in the century than the periods with which they have come to be associated. Styles that might suit American tastes, in current demands for looking glasses, would in all likelihood be seen, or sought out and acquired, by Yankee merchants in these sections. Supercargoes of ships from Philadelphia, Salem or other American ports, destined for Denmark, North Germany and Russia, may have displayed examples picked up in Ireland or England at way points. Or the reverse may have occurred on return voyages, when it is recorded that (Danish) *eglomisé* mirrors were sent home from Bilbao, a stopping point for ships bound farther southward and to the East.

Principal styles appearing in these veneered frames, generally associated with English and Irish designs, have been accepted by a native expert as characteristic of North German work. While it has not been possible to prove all of these attributions, they may at least serve to indicate a wide development, along adjoining coasts of the North and Baltic Seas, of mirror frames with variously shaped or fret-scrolled contours, and with architectural pediments.

Designs which are definitely eliminated from consideration as English are often accompanied by structural features employed in the North German and Danish areas and which are also similar to those found in some Irish work. This circumstance may indicate a transfer of such skills to Ireland, and it prompts additional caution in forming final judgments regarding origins of these mirrors.

Opinions regarding the origin of such frames, and their backboards, have been largely based on the type of pine in which they appear, often claimed as originating in New England or Pennsylvania. As a result, various Danish and North German frames have been attributed to these American states. Examinations of the frames and backboards usually reveal more knots than American craftsmen would have permitted, though the pine itself is closely similar to that used by American craftsmen.

From Brunswick in North Germany, Christian Wilmerding came to New York City in 1783 and soon opened a looking-glass store. In Philadelphia John Elliott and his sons operated several stores in which looking glasses were sold. Today both of these merchant families are considered as having been sufficiently qualified in cabinetwork, carving and gilding to have executed veneered and parcel-gilded mirror frames. The Elliotts dealt in second-hand merchandise, clothing patterns, thread, stockings, desk articles, casters, books, jewelry, buttons, painters' supplies, lumber, drugs, medicines ... and looking glasses. Wilmerding changed his store location four times between 1785 and 1795, during the same time acting as secretary of the German Society and also serving in the Militia. After a return trip to Germany he continued as a merchant for a while, and then transferred his talents to a brewery. It is remarkable that his trade card, on which he did not claim the manual skills bestowed by museum authority, prominently featured shipping cases ... and also musical instruments, which until now such authority has not credited to his hand.

There are interesting research problems for Elliott and Wilmerding enthusiasts in America: to prove that a veneered and parcel-gilded pier mirror frame was ever made by any member of the Elliott family, or by Wilmerding; to trace the course of ships, advertised as making deliveries of Elliott mirrors, to their stopping points; and to determine whether Wilmerding's mirrors came from North Germany or the British Isles.

American shipping interests in Germany were responsible for Hamburg's development as a leading port. This city was the largest and wealthiest of the ancient Hanse towns, with a population of over one hundred thousand persons at the close of the eighteenth century. The famous Derby family of Salem was represented in Hamburg by Rucker and Wortman, agents mentioned in connection with such historic cargo ships as the *Grand Turk*.

On calling at the seaports of northern Europe, supercargoes of American ships found that the production of mirror plates had reached truly advanced states. Here they augmented purchases that had been made in Ireland and England. Continental sources, however, are completely overlooked in the literature on American furniture. In *Blue Book—Philadelphia Furniture*, the author, William MacPherson Horner, Jr., after painstaking researches in an attempt to establish the presence of a similar industry here, could offer no definite facts. Singularly, a belated reference to *Hamburg, Germany,* closes this most important work, with recognition only of our export trade. Commerce is effected through the exchange of commodities—American ships were not simply freighters, they were carrying on trade. If it is finally recognized that they delivered furniture to *Hamburg, Germany,* the closing words of Horner's book, it is indeed strange that return cargoes have heretofore been given no consideration.

LIEGE AND AIX LA CHAPELLE

FURNITURE executed in the Belgian city of Liege, and in Aix la Chapelle or Aachen, deserves special mention as reflecting highly skilled approaches to French Régence, Louis XV and Louis XVI designs. Liege, the capital city in the bishopric of that name, which became a part of the Circle of Westphalia, and Aachen, an ancient free city of Germany situated near the Netherlands border, developed closely related styles. These similarities existed from the time of Louis XIV's reign to the Empire period. Furniture designs of both cities were often modeled after those which had been popular in France several decades earlier. Carved ornament and innovations in forms were also derived from Flemish, Dutch and German projects.

Richly paneled rooms of these cities were furnished with suitably carved seat furniture, tables, commodes, various types of cabinets which sometimes incorporated clocks, tall clocks, and numerous corner pieces. Such furniture is occasionally found in walnut, though more usually in natural oak with a varnish finish, while plainer pieces were painted. The carved ornament which balanced shaped moldings, giving great charm to Louis XV pieces, was not as a rule overly elaborate, but crisply cut, employing *rocaille* scrolls with folds or frills. This ornament was often asymmetrically arranged, a specialty of Aachen. *Coquillage* motives and *fleuretted treillage* panels were followed by garlands, trophies, candelabra devices, baskets of flowers, torsades of pearls, etc., in the Louis XVI style. Carving was sometimes enhanced by gilding.

Astragals in door, pilaster and side panels of china cabinets might be shaped or straight, while rococo scrollwork was sometimes combined with these, or used in additional glazed border panels. During the period of Classic influence, bowknotted garlands or stems of palm leaves were introduced to permit the more economical use of glass in small plates, though full-length glass panels are found replacing the finely carved and equally characteristic wood panels.

Design influences from Liege and Aachen penetrated adjoining German sections, especially in the duchy of Berg, while some influence from Liege reached coastal areas of Flanders and Holland, being further transmitted, through shipping contacts, as distantly as Spain.

AUSTRIA

THE DESIGN of Austrian furniture, especially prior to the Baroque period, bears a close relationship to that of South Germany, while the proximity of Italy, and in particular of Venice, is also apparent. German and Italian influences often merged in Tirolese sections, where various towns held several fairs each year, frequented by large numbers of German, Swiss and Italian traders. During the latter part of the seventeenth century there was a great influx of Italian architects, cabinetmakers, sculptors and painters, seeking better living and working conditions.

French influence developed during the first half of the eighteenth century, when the more affluent and fashionable families sent to Paris for furniture from shops of the greatest *ébénistes*. Such examples were imitated by native craftsmen, whose products, it has been claimed, were hardly distinguishable from the French pieces of the Régence and Louis XV period.

Nevertheless, like the German, Austrian furniture produced during the extended Rococo period retained much of the Baroque. This can be clearly recognized in dated pieces produced late in the century. Decided angularity appeared in curved forms, while scrolled profiles were often broken by cusps or short straight breaks in their contours. Carved ornament was generally rather heavy, though carried out with considerable style, while inlays were often rigid in effect. Inlaid bandings were favored in single light wood strips, or a darker strip enclosed by light stringing lines. Such bandings were utilized throughout the eighteenth century, in borders, or in centralized decorations, either angularly or cursively interlaced. Cube parquetry and checkered effects in borders were employed during the latter half of the century. In Austria marquetry was generally used for geometrical rather than foliage patterns. Figural ornament is seldom found in this medium.

Walnut and burl walnut were used to a considerable extent, not only native varieties but also others brought from Italy and the Rhine areas. Additional woods frequently employed were oak, maple, birch, hazel and fruitwoods. Pine was used principally for carcase work. Walnut and the fruitwoods were also utilized for secondary purposes. Cherry and yewwood came into increasing favor toward the close of the century. Austrian furniture was also popular in painted finishes, particularly in the white and gold *décor* favored in Italy and Germany.

Mahogany appeared in Viennese furniture of Louis XVI, Directoire and Empire vogues, gradually replacing walnut which was not popularly shown again until about 1830. The adoption of this imported wood, which was often given a light finish, caused some craftsmen to apply matching stains and finishes to pieces made in walnut, pearwood and other local timbers.

Austrian furniture has no particular appeal in western Europe or America today, except for pieces produced in Vienna from about 1780 to 1830. Vienna was then one of the liveliest and most magnificent cities of Europe, with over one hundred and thirty summer residences of the nobility and gentry in the populous suburb of St. Ulric. Here was the residence of the Imperial Court, and of the various foreign ambassadors. The population contained Germans, Italians, Spaniards, Dutch, Lorrainers, Swiss and many other nationals.

At this time Viennese craftsmen no longer relied upon French, German and Italian designers for inspiration. Native products, based upon the common sources of Directoire and Empire designs, were highly original, showing a good understanding of form, balance and the use of ornament in gilded bronze.

Many types of furniture that were popular in France were also found in Vienna: varieties of seat furniture, occasional tables, gueridons and *servantes*, semi-elliptical and oblong consoles, *dessertes* and commodes, bureaus and *secrétaires*. These native forms also coincided with, rather than followed, similar designs in England: dumbwaiters, sofa tables, open-shelf cabinets, and bookcases.

These pieces fit so well into modern "Regency" interiors because the mode of life in Vienna at this time closely resembled that of London. In both cities a large proportion of the population existed in comfortable circumstances. The formal architecture of their homes was accompanied by equally formal and attractive interiors, furnished to indulge elegance and leisure.

Also at this time Vienna's cabinetmaking skills developed to their highest levels. Although charges of excessive perfection may be justified, nevertheless such skills reflect the great pride taken in this manual art. Drawers and their housings were often so perfectly made and fitted that, even today, when one fair-sized drawer is pulled out and returned, the other drawers in the same bank will be propelled forward by the air force thus created. Drawer linings were delicately dovetailed, molded and finished. Intervening partitions were made flush on top, and paneled beneath with astragal moldings, applied to and concealing the four abutments. Other intricacies appeared in finely constructed interior compartments and receptacles, while laminated panels were used to prevent warping and shrinkage.

The popular use of elements, or major units of support, in the form of canephorae, eagle heads, winged caryatids, chimeras, dolphins, or shaggy legs with paw feet, may often be seen in typical Viennese productions, and in less finished Austrian work. The quality of these sculptural effects in wood and gesso will usually betoken the quality of the piece as a whole. It is apparent that lesser craftsmen did not care to let such featured work out to more specialized hands. The use of gilded elements is found in many of the finer examples, often with Egyptian head capitals carried out in either bronze work or carved wood with gesso priming.

During the Empire and Biedermeier periods Austria continued to produce both heavy and refined designs, in furniture closely paralleling the work of adjoining states, particularly Bavaria and Wurtemburg. However, Viennese designs were sometimes finer, possessing even more grace and elegance than the designs of the principal South German center of Stuttgart. During the Biedermeier period Hungarian "watered" ash came into fashion, displaying a vigorously marked figure which may be seen in the famous commode supplied by Chippendale's shop for Nostell Priory.

DENMARK

DANISH furniture of the Late Gothic and Renaissance periods displays the Teutonic origin of its peoples. Important woodworking industries in Flensburg and other principal towns were responsible for the production of many elaborate cabinet pieces. Choice of decorative elements in these times, and throughout the Baroque period in Denmark, might coincide with French or English tastes, though completed forms generally indicate closer relationships with Holland and North Germany.

Furniture centers which developed during the eighteenth century were located in Copenhagen, Altona, Lubeck, Flensburg and Kiel. Copenhagen was then the most populous city in Scandinavia. Altona, a far smaller town but still the third largest in population, was a trading center with many manufactures. Lubeck, located in the county of Wagria in Holstein, was actually an imperial city in the Diets of Lower Saxony, but is considered here as properly within the Danish sphere of interest. Flensburg and Kiel were smaller towns, the former nevertheless considered the most important in the duchy of Schleswig, the latter subject to both German and Danish alliances.

Altona is particularly associated with the production of seat furniture approximating Georgian styles, and of mirrors in more typically native designs. In addition to such productions, Lubeck was also famous for its cabinetwork.

During the middle decades of the eighteenth century Copenhagen craftsmen executed the most elaborate of Danish commodes and cabinets, richly shaped and veneered in walnut, with extravagant carving and gilded details. These were at times more embellished productions than those appearing in the Hamburg area. Their enrichment produced rather bizarre effects, even in comparison with the most striking of German pieces. Occasionally, gilded metal appliqués were substituted for the more usual carved and gilded relief ornament.

The same flamboyance is typical of many other Danish designs, which are easily recognized through acquaintance with these cabinet-pieces. Related techniques were applied to the carving of seat furniture, center and side tables, and mirror frames, not only in the main Danish island but in Schleswig Holstein.

French designs, brought from Paris by Danish craftsmen, exerted some influence. However, Danish furniture designs of the Rococo period were more greatly affected by German developments. Approximations of the Louis XV style appear in chairs, canapés, occasional tables, dressing tables, consoles and commodes. Room panelings also reflect this styling. Asymmetrical ornament frequently recalls the work of François Cuvilliés and other German architect-designers.

In Copenhagen, a city in which the foremost craftsmen congregated, productions usually displayed some native features of design throughout the Rococo and Classic periods. Danish furniture deriving from the French styles is therefore distinctive because of such renditions. Provincial designs might parallel those of similar French environs.

A decided English influence appeared during the middle decades of the eighteenth century. This is apparent in "Early Georgian" designs of chair backs, although these were often combined with typically Danish treatments of cabriole legs and seat rails. Elements of design which were adopted in Ireland are also discernible in Danish seat furniture of this time.

So much furniture was imported from England, France and Germany that an appeal on behalf of the Danish chair-makers resulted in a ban, from 1746 to 1768, on bringing in seat furniture from these countries.

In Copenhagen, "The Royal Furniture Magazine" (warehouse) was created by the Danish government in 1777 to supply furniture designs in the "modern taste," provide supplies of the choicest seasoned woods, and furnish advances on pieces to be made and sold under the seal and guarantee of the establishment. George Roentgen, brother of the more famous David, and also called an "English cabinetmaker," was connected with the magazine from 1779 to 1781.

English impetus was maintained under the later direction of Carsten Anker, a Norwegian, who was a sponsor of Simon Brotterup. The latter had studied organization and production in London for six years. He is credited with introducing English woodworking tools which had previously been unknown in Denmark. Jens Brotterup also studied in London, and later produced English types of chairs and cabinetwork in Copenhagen. The Copenhagen cabinetmakers were acquainted with *The London Cabinet-Makers' Book of Prices,* as shown by the work of Jochum Pengel.

Danish chair-makers followed English designs more closely than did the cabinetmakers. Chippendale models and later Georgian developments were accurately rendered in outlines, carved details and moldings. Generally, however, liberties were taken to accommodate local tastes, although legs and feet were often rendered in more typical English fashion than in North Germany and Sweden. A feature of some cabinetmakers, working in either English or French styles, appears in the use of similarly blocked or turned feet on all four legs of a chair, a method followed by Jens Brotterup in particular.

English-style card or tea tables were commonly used, also pembroke and sofa tables, and smaller forms for occasional use. Drop leaves were sometimes supported by fly brackets, with shaped or diagonally cut ends, but more often by plain bar lopers.

Oak and pine were both favored for carcase work in Denmark. Exposed surfaces appeared in oak, elm, walnut, birch, fruitwoods and other native timbers. With the late adoption of mahogany, coinciding with French and German importations, the exotic woods usually combined with mahogany, in veneered work, were also employed.

Many examples of Danish furniture were exported to Norway during the eighteenth century. These included the usual requirements in seat furniture, cabinet pieces and wall mirrors. Classic designs in mirror frames were of oval and oblong shapes, in which features associated with Louis XVI, Adam or Hepplewhite developments were often present. They might incorporate ribbon or laurel festoons, or filigree work supporting tiny amors.

Some particular consideration must be accorded the furniture produced in outlying districts of Denmark, in Schleswig Holstein and the neighboring islands. Schleswig was entirely subject to Denmark after 1720. Holstein was periodically subject to Danish control. In 1784 the Baltic Sea and the North or German Ocean were joined by the canal which forms a division between the two duchies. This aided American and British shipping by eliminating passages through the Skagerrack and Cattegat. Northward along the coast of Schleswig, from the town of Husum to above that of Tondern, lay the islands of Sylt, Amrom, Nordstrand, and other smaller isles, all prosperous in local activities concerned with the sea.

The populations scattered throughout this section represented a large portion of the Danish kingdom, living in modest but comfortable circumstances. Their furniture followed the styles of the large native cities or those of the countries with which they traded. Principal living rooms were paneled in oak or pine. Bedrooms were often similarly treated and furnished with richly carved bedsteads and armoires. Seat furniture frequently approximated English styles of the late seventeenth and early eighteenth centuries, while tables were of tripod or gate-leg types, or the usual Dutch and English forms for gaming and more stationary use against walls.

This mode extended to the west coast, which, with its islands, was known as North Friesland. The dialect spoken here was closer to English than any used in adjoining neighborhoods. The topography of the Frisian Isles and even the buildings and activities of the natives have been likened to those of Nantucket. Here paneled walls were often enlivened with alternate surfaces of decorative block tiles. Door lintels, frieze moldings, cabinets and shelves were all utilized to display faience and pewter. Walls were further enhanced with Friesland clocks, quill-work sconces, racks for pipes and books, hand-worked hangings and samplers.

Most important to American interest, these Frisian homes contained windsor chairs and highly decorative wall mirrors indicating early trade relations with this country. Certainly a nine-spindle, hoop-backed windsor chair, with bent armrests supported by additional spindles and two turned balusters, is a New England rather than an English type. Yet this and other scoop-seat windsor models with bowed or low flat-arched horseshoe backs were common here. Wall mirrors in walnut, mahogany or fruitwood veneers on pine, with gilded relief ornament of garlands, festoon, birds, bowknots and rosette bosses, were equally popular. (See Figs. 344-346.) Gilded brass knobs, used to support their weight, were decorative conveniences favored in Scandinavia and in America more than in England.

Earlier Danish mirrors of greater importance, with variously arched or scrolled frames, are often considered to be American "Queen Anne" or "Chippendale" examples (see Figs. 291-292). The most elaborate frames featured the flamboyant ornamentation associated with Copenhagen designs of the middle eighteenth century (see Fig. 290).

Another type of Danish mirror had delicate molded framings which enclosed a mirror border and the central beveled plate. On the reverse side of a glass panel in the angularly arched crest, and sometimes on the reverse side of the plate border, there appeared designs painted by artists of widely varying merit. Dates of these examples range from about 1750 into the nineteenth century (see Figs. 298-299). This type of mirror has been attributed to English craftsmen of the late seventeenth century. However, a more obtuse classification is that of the Metropolitan Museum of Art, which still insists upon a Chinese origin!

DANISH WEST INDIES

A CONSIDERABLE amount of furniture was delivered to, and made in, the West Indian islands (belonging to Denmark and England) during the second half of the eighteenth century and the opening decades of the following era. This has been recorded in part, in so far as the Danish islands of St. Croix and St. Thomas are concerned, but with no attempt to determine the provenance of various examples which formerly appeared in the large plantations of these islands.

Danish planters shared their islands with the Dutch, Irish and English. Furniture brought in by the Danes was largely typical of examples produced in Flensburg, the most important trading town in Schleswig. The Irish, too, are said to have patronized the furniture industry there, joining their Danish colleagues in sending West Indian timbers from which pieces were to be made and sent back to the islands.

Mahogany was the principal material sent to the homeland. It was used in the islands not only for primary but for secondary purposes. The reason is apparent in the furniture still found throughout the West Indies, in which secondary portions made of pine or other softwoods have completely deteriorated. Even the lighter and softer grades of mahogany were attacked by the larvae of the furniture beetle, proving that only the dark and heavy native variety of mahogany is immune to the ravages of this pest.

Furniture brought to St. Croix and St. Thomas by the Danes, Dutch, Irish and English, and also from America, was copied or adapted according to existing requirements. Colored natives were found to be as excellent craftsmen as those employed in our southern states, and were supervised by white foremen. It is supposed, however, that the greater amount of furniture was imported from these other areas, at least prior to the period of Empire designs.

Island styles followed the Early Georgian designs in seat furniture, tripod stands and drop-leaf tables. The latter were generally oval or oblong, with straight turned and tapered legs ending in club feet. Chippendale influence is seen in some seat furniture and in cabinet pieces fitted with drawers, or enclosed by doors of full length, or of half length with glass panels set in.

Hepplewhite and Sheraton designs were also followed, but where veneers were laid on with softwood foundations many pieces have lost complete identity through necessary restoration. However, there are gaming and dining tables, chests of drawers and larger cabinet pieces which, by their designs, prove that they were made in the islands or in Denmark. Some pieces, well kept under favorable conditions, retain secondary woods which indicate the possibility of island origins.

Empire furniture was largely influenced by Danish designs, but of greater interest to present-day collectors are the glass, or metal and glass, hurricane lights and chandeliers which accompanied this style. It is apparent from the typical forms and ornamental details of the scrolled lights and their shields that the majority were obtained from Scandinavia.

Robert Gillow, founder of the famous old Lancaster firm bearing his name, supplied furniture to the West Indies, accepting sugar, rum and cotton in return. In addition to the other sources of such imports, Sweden also provided the colonists with a small amount of furniture.

BERMUDA

FURNITURE produced in the Bermuda colony of Great Britain quite naturally followed designs which originated in the British Isles. The native cedar trees provided a principal material employed in the construction of island furniture. Seventeenth century banister-back chairs were made of oak and walnut, and mahogany was adopted in Late Georgian designs.

Seat furniture followed the more typical Queen Anne and Georgian models. There were simple rectangular frames incorporating a single pierced vase splat, or three or four verticle var splates in the back. Windsor chairs, at first imported from the American colonies, were later copied in mahogany.

Oval gate-leg tables were made with early baluster-form supports, and in Georgian designs accompanied by cabriole legs. Tray-top tables were also fashioned with cabriole legs. Mahogany tripod stands were fitted with dished tops, or, more rarely, shaped tops edged with piecrust moldings, either plain or carved.

Sideboard tables, which followed lines associated with Chippendale and Sheraton forms, were produced at the close of the eighteenth century and during the early years of the following century. Chests, bureaus and highboys were influenced by Queen Anne and Georgian developments.

Bermuda chests, in which cedar was generally used, may be found without supporting frames, or with stands in designs following Queen Anne or Chippendale styles. A most interesting feature of Bermuda work, apparently associated with a particular craftsman or his family, is seen in the use of dovetails, cut so as to form various angular patterns at the four corners of chests. These appear as key patterns, produced by cutting dovetail tenons in opposed "L" shapes, of plain or stepped figures —or in elaborate sawtooth or feather patterns effected by more intricate joining cutouts.

SWEDEN

THE SWEDISH people were little addicted to luxury when southerly countries were indulging in the elaborate furniture productions of the Renaissance. Not until the seventeenth century did furniture designing in this country adopt any particular degree of cosmopolitanism. This advance took place gradually as a result of stimulation from Holland, and to a lesser degree from France. English influence followed, in models based on Stuart designs which were continued during the opening decades of the eighteenth century.

A greater development of skills required in the production of seat furniture and cabinetwork, and in the cutting of decorative patterns on mirror plates, occurred after this time. Advances in these fields increased the appreciation and distribution of Swedish furniture between 1740 and the close of the century.

The majority of foreign craftsmen settled in Stockholm during the eighteenth century, and the capital city became noticeably influenced by French designs. From 1700 to 1740 limited numbers of Swedish master cabinetmakers were accepted into a guild established there. Increased membership during the following decades reached a peak between 1760 and 1770. The chair-makers of the city were organized as a separate guild, which was formed later than that of the cabinetmakers.

Work of these Stockholm craftsmen at first bore their manual signatures, a custom which was continued even after the introduction of *pontil* marks and labels, although later initials often served in place of full signatures. Guild marks were sometimes used in addition, while pieces which were to be exported required still another stamp.

Training acquired by Stockholm cabinetmakers in Paris was concentrated on the skills necessary to carry out the elaborate contours favored between 1740 and 1770, and also those required in laying of surface veneers. It is apparent that no concerted effort was made toward copying French Rococo or Classic designs with any degree of accuracy.

Rococo projects included bureaus, bureau-form commodes, cabinets and *medailliers*. In *bombé*, and in other serpentine structures, additional emphasis was created by pronounced curves, either where a sharp arris was employed, or the typically native, slowly rounded and involute pilaster.

In later Classic schemes daybeds and bedsteads were added to the existing upholstered forms which displayed indications of French styling. More numerous types of veneered tables and bureaus also appeared, including the *bureau plat*, *bureau à cylindre* and *secrétaire à abattant*. Larger bureaus and cabinets frequently indicated German influence, which remained less evident in other pieces.

Gilded bronze mounts were cast in richly styled

handles, escutcheons, panel surrounds and other appliqués. The appearance of identical designs, on pieces executed by various masters, indicates a common local source of supply.

Although influence from England extended to Stockholm, where some craftsmen worked in both the French and English styles, this impetus was more pronounced on the west coast. Here Goteborg was affected to a greatest extent by the English school, although the potential market of this area, based on population, totaled only a quarter of that in Stockholm.

Features associated with the popularity of walnut furniture in England appeared in Sweden during her Baroque period. It was not until the introduction of Chippendale and later Georgian styles, however, that Swedish designs showed an appreciable regard for the English school, yet English design was confined mainly to seat frames, tables and small writing pieces.

Swedish exports of furniture present an interesting study, as published by Marshall Lagerquist, *Rokokomobler*, Nordiska Museet, Stockholm, 1949. French-style seat furniture was exported from Stockholm, in pairs and complete *suites*, along with tables and desks of various types, commodes and cabinets. Numerous wall mirrors, girandoles and crystal lighting fixtures sent out from this city indicate a great development of the glass industry there. These Stockholm exports went chiefly to Swedish Pomerania, Copenhagen, St. Petersburg, Niga, Revel, Danzig, Lubeck and Hamburg.

Furniture from Goteborg was sent to northern Denmark, Norway, Canton in China, Swedish Pomerania and other sections in North Germany. In the British Isles this furniture was received in Newcastle, Hull, London, the Isle of Man and numerous Scottish towns; also at Londonderry, Belfast, Coleraine, Larne and Enniskillen in Ireland. Shipments to Spain and Portugal included deliveries made at the port of Bilbao.

NORWAY

ROMANESQUE designs and other primitive forms are largely associated with the early furniture of Norway. These were continued, combined with features of Renaissance and Baroque designs, into the seventeenth and eighteenth centuries. Compositions often paralleled Swedish provincial examples. The tree-trunk chair, or *knubstol*, a form which is occasionally represented in English and American collections today, was commonly made up to modern times.

Outside influences penetrated to Norway during the Baroque and Rococo periods as a result of trade relations with Sweden, Denmark, Holland and North Germany. Designs patterned after those of England and France are generally supplemented by features which are readily discernible as Scandinavian work, though more difficult to define as Norwegian.

With the appearance of Classic designs, Norwegian chair backs sometimes followed styles associated with the George III period, and occasionally reflected some French influence. However, like other Scandinavian work, underframes were often molded or turned in rather simple fashions.

Throughout all periods Norwegian furniture was painted and decorated with typically Scandinavian figural ornament, plant forms, names, initials, and dates of marriages or fabrication.

At the beginning of the nineteenth century appreciable progress occurred in the styling of Norwegian productions. During this time there was little influence from England or France, as the Empire and Biedermeier modes developed along typically Scandinavian and North German lines.

Norwegian mirrors, modeled after Danish designs of the so-called Queen Anne and Georgian types, were comprised of molded and arched frames surmounted by fret-scrolled crestings. Veneered examples were accompanied by others in painted lacquer finishes, and followed by varying oval shapes finished in flat paint and gilding.

During the second half of the eighteenth century, and through the Regency period, furniture was imported from England for the more important Norwegian homes, though Danish and Swedish productions were received in greater quantities.

The closest approximations of English designs occurred in native furniture produced on the west coast. This is rather strikingly illustrated by the appearance there of windsor chairs that almost duplicate an English version known by the name of a maker, "Dan Day," which were produced in Suffolk at the beginning of the nineteenth century. That these particular examples are Norwegian, rather than English, is indicated by slight variations in design, generally appearing in underframes, and in their less finished execution.

RUSSIA

RUSSIAN interest in Western culture was inaugurated with the visit of Peter the Great to Holland and England at the close of the seventeenth century. In both countries the Czar actually worked in shipyards in order to

XXI

further his knowledge and interests in maritime affairs. Founding his capital at St. Petersburg in 1703, he revisited Europe in the following decade, including Germany, Holland and France in his itinerary. Impressed with the French mode of living, he adopted French fashions. Styles of dress were changed to conform to French taste and Oriental beards disappeared

Alexandre LeBlond, a French architect, was commissioned to build the palace at Peterhof, and in 1717 left Paris for this purpose with a company of highly skilled artisans. He was joined by Nicolas Pineau, who continued LeBlond's work following the latter's demise only two years after his arrival in Russia. In turn, Russian youths from noble families were sent to England, Holland and Italy to study the arts and sciences of the West.

During the second half of the eighteenth century Russian furniture was produced in the French taste. Such work frequently manifests the presence of Italian and German craftsmen, by the profusion of carving expended on early Rococo designs and by a lack of fluidity in structural curves. Eleborately paneled and carved rooms followed this mode. A salon, which had been stored away since the early years of the century, when it was presented to Peter the Great by the King of Prussia, was then erected for the Empress Elizabeth Petronova. This admirably suited the prevailing Russian *décor*.

More accurate renditions of the French school eventually appeared, executed in mahogany, ebony, violetwood, palisander and *citronnier*. Inlaid decorations in parquetry, marquetry and nacre work were accompanied by gilded carvings or *bronze doré* mounts.

Stockholm deliveries to Russia, from 1744, are listed by Marshall Lagerquist as gueridons, French-model commodes, writing and dressing tables, and secretaries, while keyboard musical instruments and various other items were also shipped to St. Petersburg, Reval and Riga. A large quantity of mirrors which were received in St. Petersburg appeared in gilded, lacquered or polished finishes. Later, furniture was delivered by David Roentgen, while Paris examples were supplied by Jean-Henri Riesener and Georges Jacob, along with bronzes by Caffieri and Gouthiere.

Catherine the Great was so impressed on seeing a book devoted to a study of the Roman baths, published in 1772 by the Scottish architect, Charles Cameron, that he was summoned to the court and commissioned to work for the Queen. During Cameron's activities in Russia, from 1779 to 1796, he introduced his designs in architecture and furniture in the Palace of Pavlosk, at Tsarkoe Selo, and in lesser projects for the nobility. His death in Russia is confirmed only by the sale there, in 1812, of the library of the "late Charles Cameron."

Cameron's architectural projects offer some parallels to the work of his countryman, Robert Adam, who is known to have designed a harpsichord for the Empress. Other compositions were apparently influenced by Sir William Chambers' projects in the Chinese taste. Painted effects were carried out principally by Italian artists.

Decorative mediums employed by Cameron reveal a versatility of choice, including marble, alabaster, porphyry, agate, malachite, lapis lazuli and other semi-precious stones. He also favored tinted glass, mirror panels, mural paintings, stucco ornament, porcelain and faience. Jasper wares were supplied to Catherine the Great by Josiah Wedgwood, as one of his *most regular and important customers*.

Seat furniture and side tables designed by Cameron, and executed in Russian shops, often achieved the same results that are seen elsewhere in the assimilation of both French and English designs of the later style periods, thus paralleling some German and Swedish examples developed under these two influences, and amply illustrating this phase of interrelation.

An interesting development occurred at the close of the eighteenth century. The popularity of designs which had been seen in chairs received from the Jacob atelier was responsible for the accurate copying of these models in St. Petersburg. Representing the period in which Jacob was subject to French influence, these designs were therefore transposed from London to Paris, and thence to St. Petersburg.

At least one British furniture shop must have been operating in Russia when Sheraton's *Drawing Book* was published, as "Dillon, Cabinetmaker, Russia," is listed therein as a subscriber.

HOLLAND

WITH the establishment of her great trade in the East, and in the West Indies, Holland rapidly became the richest nation in Europe. This wealth was not centralized in the larger cities, but extended to landowners of outlying districts, where it was still apparent after the decline of Dutch power in the late seventeenth century and a final collapse during the ensuing decades.

Designs of native furniture are by no means graceful, facile, subtle or dainty. They are, however, often decidedly virile, presenting handsome effects that may approach a certain delicacy in the more refined compositions. There is always a feeling of sturdiness and restraint, the latter quality extending to elaborate sculptured features. Sobriety and dignity and, wherever possible, economy and usefulness in everyday life, were more often achieved by Dutch designers and craftsmen.

Throughout the seventeenth century, designs in Holland inspired work of all neighboring countries, particularly in northern Europe and England. Although Holland had previously derived some influence from France, this impetus became more active during the eighteenth century, when, after 1730, furniture and decorations in Holland were propelled by French Rococo developments. This influence later spread as far north as Friesland, where the more important edifices were richly paneled and furnished to suit the mode. Louis XVI designs were also closely followed, while Directoire and Empire projects in Holland were sometimes fashioned with principal elements derived through French motivation.

Interpretations of French seat furniture were more accurately rendered than cabinetwork, while artisans concerned with both branches of furniture-making continued to work in native styles throughout the periods of Gallic influence.

Dutch lacquer cabinets, copied from examples obtained in China and Japan, were popular in Holland and England during the late seventeenth and early eighteenth centuries. These were mounted upon gilded or silvered stands, designed and carved in native styles, or indicating French Louis XIV and Régence influences. Both cabinets and stands of this type are often mistaken for English products today. Throughout the balance of the eighteenth century, lacquer techniques in Holland continued to develop, approaching advances made in France and Germany, in contrast to the quality of this work commonly found in English specimens.

Holland had been largely responsible for the rise of furniture crafts in England during the seventeenth century, and continued to exert influence in this direction through the following decades. However, despite her commercial ties with England, and the emigration of Dutch workmen to that country, English furniture designs never affected those of Holland to any appreciable degree. This is additionally remarkable, as English furniture was imported during the eighteenth century. These importations, and others obtained from France, were marked with a prescribed stamp, which appears in the form of a coroneted shield enclosing a row of crosses, and flanked by the letters "J" and "G."

Furniture which has been lightly regarded as "William and Mary," "Queen Anne" or "Early Georgian" was executed during extended periods of popularity in Holland, often accompanied by later elements of ornamentation. These baroque forms will be found with rococo, or even classic details. The fixed rule, that a piece of furniture be dated only according to its latest feature of design, is often disregarded in ascribing dates to such examples. This phenomenon is particularly apparent in seat furniture, where seventeenth century forms were continued well into the following era, while "Queen Anne" features appear in Dutch examples made during the second half of the eighteenth century.

Design influences from Holland penetrated far into the eastern and southern states of Germany, and through Scandinavia, during the first half of the eighteenth century. Examples produced under this influence have been readily accepted as of Dutch provenance, adding further to a misunderstanding which has also accepted Irish examples, and those executed in England by Dutch craftsmen, in the category of Dutch furniture.

As the Dutch were carriers for much of the trade in Europe, cargoes of exotic timbers brought home by their ships served to introduce these in neighboring vicinities, and thus to affect local productions of furniture. While palisander, ebony and lignum-vitae were imported during the seventeenth century, mahogany did not come into general use in Holland, France, Scandinavia or Germany until the middle of the following era. This delayed adoption, on the Continent, of such a superior medium for the construction and preservation of furniture, is sometimes of service in considering examples which are related to English designs.

In addition to other distantly acquired timbers, such as rosewood, padouk, satinwood, etc., the Dutch utilized oak, walnut, elm, ash, pine, beech, sycamore and fruitwoods in their furniture. Elaborate marquetry work and banded inlays were enhanced with tortoise shell, ivory, brass, pewter and silver.

The Hollanders also bought up large quantities of timber on the Continent, much of which passed through Dordrecht, a center for this trade, with many sawmills operating there during the eighteenth century. Hindeloopen mariners supplied additional timbers from Scandinavia to Amsterdam and smaller ports. Native supplies of forest trees, never abundant in Holland, had become so depleted during the nineteenth century as to consist of *only a few plantations of oak, beech and elm, clumps of pine on the links or sand drifts, and rows of willow and poplar along the banks of canals.*

Regulation in Holland stipulated use of oak for secondary work in veneered pieces made by *cabinet-workers*, a medium also favored for carved mirror frames and architectural treatments, though here linden and pine are also to be found. The use of pine, imported or domestic, together with other soft whitewoods, was restricted to a separate guild of cabinetmakers, referred to as *whiteworkers*, for constructing pieces that were to be finished with painted or lacquered decorations.

DUTCH COLONIAL FURNITURE

A LARGE quantity of furniture was made for the early Dutch settlers in their colonial possessions. Such pieces are often distinctive in their native designs and materials, and were often constructed with wood pegs without the use of glue, while others were copied directly from Dutch models. Small furniture centers existed in Java, where a principal trading station was situated at Batavia, in Ceylon, the Coromandel Coast and in South Africa.

Pieces brought home to Holland during the eighteenth century are found with stamped marks in the form of an "O" and "C" pierced through from beneath by a larger "V" (*Verenigde Oost-Indische Compagnie*), and accompanied by the year date of dispatch via ships of the (United) Dutch East India Company.

Ebony was a principal material, as well as *Maba ebenus*, which varies from true ebony but is accepted today as such. Teak, padouk, sappan wood which somewhat resembles Brazil wood, camphor wood, bullet wood, bloodwood, stinkwood, sandalwood, calamander and other native timbers were also utilized. Silver and base metals were fashioned into mounts for cabinet pieces, often following Japanese and Chinese patterns in hinges and lockplates. Ivory, and inlays of ivory, were especially favored in India.

Jan van Riebeck was sent out, in 1652, to found a settlement at the Cape of Good Hope, as a stopping point for shipping from the Far East. Craftsmen brought from Batavia, Ceylon and India showed particular partiality for the use of the local stinkwood, and yellow wood of the pine family. Native "oaks" and olivewood, as well as teak and satinwood, were also favored. Stinkwood, though scarce today, and regardless of a pronounced odor when freshly cut, is still regarded as the best of South African timbers for furniture-making. Somewhat resembling walnut, this wood is of a similar color, with a slightly reddish tone. Native olivewood, harder than European olive, is sometimes known as ironwood, a term often applied to exceptionally hard or heavy timbers. Ebony, satinwood and ivory were used in later work for rather reserved inlays.

Use of such woods will generally characterize furniture of the Cape Colony that was produced in typical Dutch designs, forsaking use of popular Indian and other Eastern motifs. It is well to remember, however, that various "Indian" woods were imported and used in Holland, particularly in seat furniture designed and ornamented in colonial fashions.

It is claimed that "Burgomaster" chairs, which in recent times have become desired specimens in England, America and Germany, originated in this colony during the time of van Riebeck—a slightly prejudiced tradition. However, around the turn of the seventeenth century the form became popular in Holland, and was copied, along with other styles of seat furniture and tables derived from Africa and the East, until the middle of the eighteenth century when rococo elements were introduced in these frames.

Further north along the east coast of Africa, in Kenya, furniture was also produced, allied to that of the Cape Colony. From the late seventeenth century, designs executed in Kenya were influenced by Dutch, Portuguese, and Portuguese East Indian work, and later also by impetus received from England.

The "kidney bean" cabochon, a popular carved motif in furniture made throughout the Netherlands, and in Pennsylvania, also appears in African colonial work where it has been associated with the native *korosho* nut.

Importance of Dutch trade with the Far East is responsible for a large amount of the lacquer furniture executed there for the European market, as well as for the reception in Europe of typically Japanese and Chinese furniture during the seventeenth and eighteenth centuries. Much of that which was specially made along European lines, and is believed to have been copied from English designs, was made to Dutch orders and after Dutch models.

Principal Dutch factories were maintained at Canton in China, and at Deshima in Japan. The

Hollanders were the only Europeans permitted to maintain residence in the latter islands after 1638.

Records exist in Amsterdam of Oriental artists in lacquer (*Japanish Verlakker*) working there in the late seventeenth and eighteenth centuries. The inferior cabinetwork, apparent in many of the exports from China, produced complaints which finally resulted in the dispatch of a Dutch joiner to supervise such matters. In contrast to suppositions that English furniture was sent to China for decorating in lacquer, some few unfinished pieces of Dutch furniture are recorded as having been handled in this manner.

CHINA AND THE PHILIPPINES

FAR EASTERN furniture, executed under the influence of European designs, is in general strongly characteristic, but in some instances may approach these designs rather closely. Native materials and joining methods usually distinguish even the closest parallels, which may be found in examples made for European residents. Perhaps one of the closest approximations to Western design appeared here recently in a Chippendale settee, carefully following an English outline in its upholstered frame, but with the underframing made of camphor wood.

Native varieties of pine, oak, ash, elm, cedar, beech and walnut may appear in principal surfaces or structural elements of Chinese furniture. Other likely timbers are ebony, teak, rosewood, sandalwood, satinwood, maple, box, cherry and other fruitwoods. Teak is widely believed to be one of the darker and heavier woods, which is incorrect. It is lighter in color and weight than rosewood, with which it is often confused in late productions.

Oriental authorities are occasionally perplexed by calligraphic markings which appear on assembled elements of lacquer furniture, generally in reserves left for this purpose. These vary from usual Chinese or Japanese characters, which indicate the positions of drawers, etc., and cannot be directly associated with either country. Examples on which they appear have followed Chinese forms, and it is possible that these represent collaborations by Chinese artisans, and those of more southerly areas, working in the same or differing production centers.

Other Far Eastern furniture may give more definite evidence of assembly at two different trading points. It is known that much work in lacquer, for export, was carried on in Tongking, Indo China, in addition to the work of Canton and Nanking. Trading factories at various points on the mainland and in the East Indian islands were also capable of executing special work. The lacquer cabinet and stand illustrated in Fig. 249 represents an amalgamation of this type, the cabinet produced in China, the stand at some intermediate shipping point.

A photograph of this cabinet and stand was shown to a dealer who had handled and seen thousands of specimens of Chinese furniture, in the belief that the claw-and-ball feet were derived from the West, not from China. One of many theories advanced more than a generation ago was that this type of foot was introduced in Europe through Spanish and Portuguese contacts with China. However, this was not proven by visual demonstration, and it gave no cognizance to appearances of the claw-and-ball foot in the West during Romanesque times.

The authority agreed that no connection existed between this type of foot and that of a Chinese dragon grasping a pearl. He also stated that this Western form was not adopted in China until first used in Europe, and then only in furniture supplied for this market.

When the role of expert prevents one from permitting such inquiries as inconsistent with assumed authority, a chance to expand knowledge has been eliminated. Had the experts responsible for a "Chinese" label on the mirror mentioned in connection with Fig. 298 inquired of their own authorities on Chinese art, they would have been informed that no such work was ever executed in China. Had they consulted dealers in Portuguese, Spanish or Italian antiques, regarding "Bilbao" mirrors, they would have been similarly informed.

Furniture produced in the Philippine Islands during the eighteenth century was partially affected by Chinese and Spanish influences. These are seen in carved details following the Chinese taste, and in stellate devices which are reminiscent of Moorish effects, inlaid in bone or mother-of-pearl and occasionally in silver. Of the few examples which appear in the West, sideboard tables indicate a former popularity, and are amply proportioned in length and space.

Late Georgian influence is noticeable in some Philippine chairs with caned back and seat panels, or with backs containing radial bar splats. These were accompanied by semi-circular side tables, which also served as the end sections of dining tables. As in other Eastern colonies which were

XXV

maintained during the nineteenth century, later productions gradually disclosed the effects of the Victorian era.

The most popular timber of the Philippines was the native *narra* wood. This varies greatly in color, from light golden and brown tones through shades of light or dark red, and may show ripples or fine mottles such as are found in mahogany. *Narra* is moderately hard and heavy, and excellent to work with in the production of furniture.

Ireland

THE long periods of discord and strife in Ireland are recorded by many historians who pass over progress made during the early part of the eighteenth century. This neglect is partially responsible for a general belief that Ireland prospered only after the middle of that century. However, in challenge of this long-established belief, and corroboration of an early eighteenth-century development of prosperity, the erection of public edifices and monuments have been cited. These include the statue of William III in 1701, Dublin Castle in 1720, the statue of George I in 1720, the Linen Hall in 1728, and the Bank of Ireland in 1729. During these years Irish silverware, formerly supplied to the monasteries, was also produced for communal use, an additional indication of a society which, in supporting this form of luxury, would undoubtedly extend equal interest to its household furniture.

One and a quarter million persons comprised the population of Ireland in 1700, a figure far in excess of many Continental states then producing fine furniture, and one which was reached in Scotland only at the close of the century, when Ireland's population had increased to around four million.

Dublin was of course the principal city to foster the furniture crafts, and where chair- and cabinet-makers from the Continent and England would be most likely to settle. There was a considerable increase in the city population after 1711, a further sign of prosperity, and it has been accepted as a hypothesis here that, coinciding with the period of Holland's decline, artisans connected with various phases of furniture-making in that country, and from other areas of the Continent, emigrated to continue their skills among this increased population.

Even less is known about the smaller Irish towns, where furniture is concerned, than about Dublin. However, the fact that Abraham Roentgen is known to have found use for his highly trained skills in Galway, a town with only a fraction of the population of Dublin, is important in recording an accessible industry there, already well established before the middle of the eighteenth century.

It is known that this industry in Dublin had advanced during the first half of the century to a stage where furniture was delivered to towns situated along the west coast of the principal island section of Great Britain. It is, therefore, certain that a considerable quantity was supplied within the city and its environs, but the full extent of this production will never be disclosed. Sizable manufactories existed, however, long before the division of English social activities into "London and Dublin Seasons," and were apparently fostered by increasing numbers of permanently settled residents and visiting landowners. Further conjecture might safely assume that particularly skilled developments would offer ready and economic competition to London enterprises, under acquisitive consideration by these permanent residents, and possibly by those whose visits were seasonal.

Study of these developments might be continuously retarded by present emphasis on Irish designs as typical in their employ of grimacing masks, heavy festoons, ribbed square feet and similar excesses. These features are recognized by all today, except our Metropolitan Museum, and are representative of a local school, still unlocated by native authorities but of little interest in comparison with more refined Irish work.

Additional hindrance has been offered by the vast amount of Irish furniture which has been removed to England and America, and even to the Continent, leaving very little as native evidence. In response to inquiries made during the present research, the Belfast Museum was able to supply only a single illustration of a definitely ascribed Irish example, this being a side table of the characteristic lion-mask and satyr-head type. The National Museum of Ireland, in Dublin, explained that *no decisive criteria have been evolved for discriminating what is Irish and what is English.*

A knowledge of English furniture is undoubtedly essential in ascertaining style developments in Ireland. However, further and possibly greater aids may be obtained through an understanding of work in Holland and neighboring Continental areas, and that which developed in America between 1730 and 1790.

The period during which William III and Queen Anne styles were followed in England actually extended beyond these reigns by two decades at least. Craftsmen who had come over from Holland were still responsible for producing a considerable portion of this later work. After 1735 their presence is less apparent in English work that was carried out in mahogany, but becomes more evident in that of Ireland, where walnut furniture continued in favor for several decades after the introduction of mahogany.

At this time, and during the third quarter of the century, the similarity to contemporary Dutch examples, of some Irish seat furniture and cabinetwork produced under this influence, is quite remarkable. Illustrations of such pieces cause immediate attention in Holland, contrasting to a general lack of interest in examples derived from typical English designs.

In some instances walnut tables and cabinets in the Queen Anne taste, which may have been produced in Ireland, receive this attention, and might be considered as of Dutch provenance except for the appearance of pine in secondary parts. However, a desire to establish a considerable number of such pieces, especially bureaus and secretaries, in the category of Irish furniture must await further proofs of Irish rather than English origin.

Irish designs were transferred to America between 1730 and 1740, being continued in work of later emigrants from that country, and obtaining a wider adoption through the popularity they received. This interest was centered in Philadelphia, where Plunkett Fleeson, upholsterer, advertised his late arrival from Dublin in 1739, giving *second* importance to London in recommending himself. With the increasing numbers of Irish-trained craftsmen who appeared throughout the following decades, Irish designs were actively transmitted in Pennsylvania, New Jersey, New York and New England. The same influence is also apparent in many examples of furniture produced in the South, where in 1786 James McCormick of Alexandria advertised his *long experience in some of the first shops of England and Ireland.*

American Queen Anne styles in seat furniture often appear with the so-called "Dutch" or "web" foot, adopted from Ireland. Other Irish features were combined in cabriole-leg frames with solid or pierced splats, and were continued in later straight-legged types. Such models are often found with splats or cross slats pierced in exact duplication of Irish fret patterns, which were not directly inspired—in Ireland or America—by English designs. In some instances designs of Irish chairs, complete in all details, were copied in Philadelphia —if even a fraction of documented and published examples are correctly assigned.

These Irish-American designs also appear in tripod tables with tilting tops, though the turned colonnettes of "bird-cage" supports were generally given richer baluster shapings in this country. They occur in oblong tables of various types made prior to or during our Chippendale period, especially those which were popular for serving tea or playing cards, and for use in stationary positions. In chests of drawers and cabinets they may be seen as variations of English themes, often concentrated on the handling of pilasters, bracket feet, astragals, and the treatment of cornices and pediments. Irish types of gadrooning, and leaf- or fret-carving frequently accompany these forms.

Among the numerous pieces of Irish furniture which have arrived in America, many of the earliest to be received were pier mirrors with parcel-gilded walnut frames. These preceded, and were later joined by, others of similar nature executed in mahogany. They were followed by still others which were entirely gilded, while *eglomisé* panels were added at the turn of the eighteenth century —when Denmark, Germany, Holland and France were active in this same supply.

Most of these imported mirrors, which were welcomed here in the shortage of fine framings and large mirror plates, have remained in America since the time of their manufacture and shipment to this country. Such examples should have great interest to collectors of this nation, for they not only indicate the requirements and tastes of our forebears, but through long periods of naturalization they have certainly become American.

The more obvious characteristics of Irish design do not present the interest which can be obtained from more detailed study. In many cases London projects were closely approximated in Ireland, and in such instances it may be that appearance of certain improprieties alone will distinguish these productions. The liberties taken indicate a lack of acquaintance with, or indifference to, established conventions by a certain number of craftsmen.

These licenses often result in vagaries which would not be condoned in England, or in principal furniture centers on the Continent. A particular caprice appears in the use of gadroons running in reverse directions to the accepted disposition, as seen in Figs. 709, 759, 760 and 766. Another departure from established custom may be seen where carved leaf scrolls are extended downward on the knees of cabriole supports, rather than in the usual upward curve, a license which appears in Figs. 693, 735, 752 and 758.

The high standard of carving and of cabinetwork, found in many specimens of Irish furniture, has been long recognized in America. This recognition has been granted in part by skilled artisans, engaged here in restoring American furniture, through whose hands numerous Irish pieces have therefore passed. The accomplishments of Irish craftsmen in these fields are comparable to their interpretations of design. While some work may parallel that of London, in other instances Continental techniques are present, or evidences which indicate little regard for perfection.

Irish seat furniture sometimes appears with a heavy coating of black finishing material, or remains of this material, apparently used to complement the darker grades of mahogany. Gilding was occasionally employed on painted beechwood frames of the lion-mask period, and later in the century. Settees were fashioned with only four legs, when their length required at least an additional front support to accord with proper tenets of design and construction. These seat frames might be fitted with open bar braces at junctions of the rails, with corner blocks, or they might remain entirely unbraced. Where braces or blocks appear they are found in oak, beech or walnut. Slip seats and strainers, or seat stretchers, were made in these same woods or in red, white or pitch pine. Beech might be employed in rear seat rails, the cores of splats, and for rear uprights. Ash was also utilized for rear seat rails, or for all rails when mahogany facings were employed. In Continental habit, these Irish frames were sometimes stamped with the initials of makers.

The use of walnut during the second half of the eighteenth century, as a principal or secondary wood, and the retention of other features of construction which had been discontinued in London, such as running drawer bottoms from front to rear, distinguish some cabinetwork. An account of Philadelphia commerce, written in 1754, indicates a specialization in the supply of walnut—*To Ireland are sent . . . walnut boards*. Oak, and red or white pine, combined or separately employed, appears in Irish structural work. When London methods were closely followed, partitions of full depth separated the long drawers of case pieces.

Although classic designs were adopted in Ireland toward the close of the eighteenth century, earlier projects were still continued. These often contain few evidences of late work, though in some instances cabinet pieces may reveal interior structural features which became general only at this time. Features of this type, or those of earlier development, may at times be overspread with a wash of "Sheraton pink" staining material. Sycamore and satinwood veneers were introduced during the late eighteenth century, together with a number of the rarer woods generally employed in marquetry decorations accompanying these schemes. Furniture was also painted and decorated in the classic taste, though the full extent of this work has been but briefly sketched up to the present time, and various pieces finished in plain colors or more elaborate effects are still to be confirmed as Irish productions.

The study of furniture designs requires attention not only to matters of usual historical and geographic significance, but is aided by statistics concerning the populations of regions where furniture was manufactured, exported and imported. Consideration of population totals, alone, may indicate some improbabilities in the amount of furniture generally believed to have been produced in certain countries or states during the eighteenth century. Such consideration has directed the tracing of a large number of designs according to Irish developments, which had previously received speculation as to Continental origins, based on features associated with Baltic and North Sea areas.

Census taking was a difficult procedure in the eighteenth century, when various prejudices against the counting of families existed, while figures offered by contemporary or later writers often prove to be incorrect. The most accurate early records were made pursuant to acts of the English Parliament, passed in 1815 to determine the population and ascertain *the increase and diminution thereof* in Ireland, and in 1801, to determine the population of England. While these records do not permit a completely parallel view of the subject, they may serve very roughly to emphasize the relative size of the largest cities in the two countries at about these dates.

This comparison, apparently prejudiced here in favor of Ireland, shows Dublin, with a population of 176,610 persons, larger than that of the city of

London within and without the Walls (129,528) but smaller when the City of Westminster is added, increasing this total to 282,800. Cork, with 64,349 souls, was larger than Bristol with Barton Regis Hundred (63,645), Macclesfield (56,437), Leeds (53,160), Norwich (36,832), Bath (32,200), Nottingham (28,861), or Newcastle on Tyne (28,366). Waterford and Galway, with 25,467 and 24,684 persons, respectively, were each larger than Exeter (17,398), or Chester (15,052), and over twice the size of Oxford (11,694), Worcester (11,352), or Lancaster (9,030) where the Gillow furniture factory had already acquired a widely known reputation.

Comparison of populations in Ireland and its principal cities from 1700 to 1800, with those of the entire group of American states developing during this period, may interest American collectors. There were only about 275,000 inhabitants here in 1700, when it is supposed that there were about a million and a quarter in Ireland. Despite our rapid growth, it was not until the closing years of the century that the combined population of the American states became equal to that of Ireland. Both countries were largely rural and supported from the soil, but while American towns were still very small in 1800, Dublin is then said to have contained about 200,000 inhabitants, twice the number reached in New York City as late as 1820. (In 1800 Hamburg, Copenhagen and Stockholm, all important centers of furniture manufactures and exports, contained far smaller populations than Dublin, 100,000, 90,000 and 80,000, respectively.)

By the close of the eighteenth century Ireland's sea trade was also relatively extensive, being reckoned at £10,000,000 in 1800, most of which was accounted for by exportations. The amount of furniture which was included in these exports cannot be assessed today. It may be accepted, however, that Irish furniture was exported to the principal island section of Great Britain, to northern areas of the Continent, and to America. How far southward in Europe interest in Irish furniture may have reached is indicated by the appearance, in Spain and Portugal, of side tables which follow the lines of the more easily recognized types produced around the middle of the eighteenth century. These tables feature the characteristic frieze of scant depth, and swelling, deeply valanced apron curving into cabriole legs with claw-and-ball feet. In place of lion or satyr masks, oak leaf and acorn festoons, etc., they are carved with more delicate foliage ornament, in the Iberian taste.

Structural Methods and Materials

ENGLAND is the sole country where fairly standardized tectonic methods were followed, and where these may be recorded with any particular degree of accuracy. Recognition of these methods has resulted in various detailed descriptions throughout the past twenty-five years. This has been considered impractical in Central Europe because of many confusions resulting from the wide and constant movements of workers; also, no serious attempts have been made in this direction in France or America. To enter lengthy and reiterative comparisons, according to notes taken during this particular study, would serve no greater purpose here than to emphasize the importance of design.

In regard to French furniture, a native authority has pointed out that other craftsmen were equally skilled in manual ability, having employed all technical procedures prior to their adoption in France; moreover, that developments in surface work, such as lacquer decoration, metal and wood marquetry, were motivated by Italy, Germany and the Netherlands.

Paris was a center on which artisans converged from Italy, Austria, Germany, the Netherlands and Scandinavia; while a far smaller proportion of French craftsmen left to work in other countries, as far distant as Russia. Fine work of centers other than Paris, compared with that of native Parisian craftsmen, is often scarcely distinguishable, and this may also apply in the production of *meubles usuels*. Joining methods, structural features, such as partitions employed between drawers of commodes, and choice of secondary woods, while useful to some extent in determining the origin of furniture, are not as definitive as *design*.

It may be said that oak was more generally used for construction in France than elsewhere on the Continent, with the exception of Holland. Pine, as a satisfactory medium for secondary use, especially in fashioning the built-up cores of serpentine and *bombé* pieces, was universally favored. More typical French methods may be observed in the use of rabbets on lower surfaces of drawer bottoms, rather than chamfers, permitting a more or less flush finish with the sides and back; and in veneering the inner surfaces of drawer fronts. However, these methods were not entirely confined to French practice, but were sometimes spread by Parisian-trained cabinetmakers.

In Lucotte's *Menuisier en Meubles* no particularly identifiable characteristics of construction are shown. While all members of seat and case frames are illustrated, these were apparently offered with emphasis on design and material. Principal framings are depicted as simply tenoned, with bracing bars fitted in by dovetail terminals. Mortice pins are rounded and tapered to points, forming actual trenails rather than the untapered pegs more generally used. Interiors of work shops are pictured as set up for making seat frames and cabinetwork under the same roof.

Roubo, a fine working *maître ébéniste*, in 1768 and 1775 showed more complete plans and elevations, tenon joins, metal screws and trenails; the latter were repeated in plates taken directly from Lucotte. It is only in the special plates devoted by Roubo to highly skilled and intricate joining methods that such techniques become distinctive, and the suggestions offered would of necessity, if carried out, be concealed from later observation within the woodwork.

The British Isles received craftsmen from Italy, the Netherlands, various municipalities of Germany, and from Scandinavia, to work and study there. In turn, independent masters and apprentices from England worked in northern areas of the Continent. These exchanges are partially responsible for the fact that English systems of chair-making and cabinetwork were sometimes more closely followed in Germany and Scandinavia than in America.

In chair-making, one particular English development often characterizes such work, although sometimes employed elsewhere. This is found in the use of square blocks as terminals for the turned traverse member of a stretcher, and similar median blockings on the two lateral members. These butted together and formed a more satisfactory joining method than when either or both blockings were eliminated, a practice generally favored on the Continent, especially in Holland, and in America.

The fact that a chair splat is set into a rear seat rail *without* the use of a separate shoe piece does not always indicate modern work. While antique splat-back chairs which were made in England invariably possess this separate feature, other examples, more or less following the English taste, were constructed by Continental chair-makers, and those working in Ireland, without its use. English seat frames are often found with short, squared bars serving to brace the corners. This type of open corner bar, contrasting with solid triangular blocks which were also used for the same purpose, may be found in seat furniture of Holland, Denmark and North Germany. Continental frame-makers often stamped their products with identifying initials, and numbered sets of chairs by chisel cuts in incorrect Roman numerals, such as IIII or VIIII. Similar notations are found in work performed in Ireland, and sometimes in England.

Tables and seat furniture of simple frame construction lack the determinative structural features sometimes present in pieces incorporating a greater number of elements. However, while wood pegs utilized in doweling these frames were often left projecting in Continental work, the English invariably cut their pegs short, to leave no projections.

Where tables have been fitted with drop leaves, their supports may supply some identifying clues. The English fly bracket, with ogee-shaped terminal, was not adopted in America, where this support followed the German and Scandinavian form with diagonally cut end, and generally with square teeth forming the wood hinges. In contrast to developments in America, some Continental craftsmen did adopt the English type bracket. In Denmark drop-leaves were often supported by lopers, simple square rods pulling straight out beneath the leaves.

English case pieces with long drawers were often supplied with separating partitions between the drawers. Elimination of such partitions was the general rule in America, another choice in marked contrast to English training. On the Continent their avoidance or use, in full or part depth, was discretionary, and is indicative neither of quality nor of origin. Contrary to certain opinions, full-length partitions may appear in eighteenth century Dutch work.

Drawer construction in Holland presents some characteristic features. Often sides were set into rabbets cut in the drawer front and secured only by nails. When dovetails were used, these were sometimes combined with simple nailed construction. Through-dovetails continued in use concurrently with those of stopped type. (The stopped dovetail was favored in England throughout the greater part of the eighteenth century, until, toward its close, the through-dovetail reappeared in some work.)

German cabinetmakers often finished drawer sides with a rounded top edge, or molded this edge with a double beading, a feature which is noticeable in American block-front, and other case pieces. In South Germany and Austria this molding work was sometimes continued on the traverse members.

A considerable amount of German furniture, and a very large proportion of that produced in Scandinavia, is found with the pine cores of drawer fronts exposed on top, a method followed in England only during the early production of walnut furniture. This lack of finished work is found in pieces executed by the greatest Swedish masters, and was sanctioned in both early and later work.

In French cabinetwork, and Continental work in general, drawers were furnished with long locks in which the mechanisms were operated through keyholes placed in central positions of the drawer fronts. The standard English square lock, adopted late in the seventeenth century, caused the keyhole to appear nearer the top edge of the drawer front. Occasional examples of English cabinetwork, some attributed to designs by Robert Adam, display central keyholes, which may appear in square locks, but as a rule this will denote a product of the Continent or Ireland.

The Dutch utilized both long and short locks, the latter form coming into vogue during the early part of the eighteenth century, spreading to some extent from Holland to Scandinavia and North Germany. Later in the century square locks employed in Potsdam, Dresden and Leipzig furniture were received from England.

Early locks were fashioned with wards, or projecting metal ridges, as obstacles against operation by keys without corresponding notches, features which have been continued in use to the present day. In 1774 Robert Barron, an Englishman, invented a lock which combined with these wards two double-acting tumblers to impede action of the bolt. Levers and slides which eliminated use of wards altogether were employed by Joseph Bramah a short time later. The "lever lock" thus developed found favor in England from the close of the eighteenth century, being distinctively labeled by stamping with a die.

Bramah's specifications for an early lever lock were submitted in 1784, and he was later recorded as making the finest locks in England, being mentioned with praise by Thomas Sheraton. The name of the firm he founded will be seen on many original locks, appearing as "I" BRAMAH, etc. The firm name was J. Bramah in 1800, J. Bramah & Son in 1813, Bramah & Sons from 1821 to 1836, Bramah & Prestige from 1837 to the middle of the century, and Bramah & Co. afterwards.

Barron's made and stamped locks during the end of the eighteenth, and in the early nineteenth, century. Jeremiah Chubb, apparently in collaboration with his brother, Charles, invented a detector lock in 1818, using six or more levers, protected by a detector lever which was employed to throw the mechanism out of kilter with an attempt to pick it. The manufacturing firm was known as J. & C. Chubb in 1818, in 1824 and 1849 it appeared as C. Chubb, or Charles Chubb, and in 1852 and 1860 issues of the *London Directory* as C. Chubb & Son.

Lever locks gradually came to be made by a large number of firms, and were stamped with such descriptive legends as SAFETY, PATENT LEVER LOCK, SECURE 4 LEVER, SECURE HAND-MADE FOUR LEVER LOCK, and HOBBS & CO. MACHINE MADE LEVER. Most of these have appeared on rather late examples of nineteenth-century furniture.

Crowns were stamped on some early lever locks, despite opinions to the contrary. Bramah employed this representation on a model with his original form of mechanism, labeled I BRAMAH, and PATENT. Crowns were repeated during the reigns following that of George III, with the identifying monograms of WR and VR, for William and Victoria Rex. Cabinet pieces of Sheraton and Regency designs are sometimes found with original locks bearing the latter monogram, affording additional proof of the late production of such designs.

From the earliest times, timber used in the making of furniture was cut with a pit saw. In its operation one end of this long saw was worked from a position in a pit beneath the trunk or balk. This method was continued in many areas up to the last decades of the nineteenth century. Frame saws were also operated by two men, in cutting such balks as were stocked by shop owners, from the Renaissance to the later decorative periods.

It is believed that large timber saws, propelled by water power and working with a reciprocal motion, were operated in Europe as early as the fourteenth century. Sawing machines are recorded throughout a large portion of Europe during the fifteenth and sixteenth centuries, and in England during the following century. Mills then operated

XXXI

several saws in gangs, parallel to each other. A Swedish machine of this type, operating in 1653, was worked by a twelve-foot water wheel giving action to as many as seventy-two saws.

Parallel kerf marks, sometimes found on boards cut by mill saws, should be distinguished from later evidences left by band saws, which were introduced during the second half of the nineteenth century.

The circular saw is claimed by the Dutch. It was developed in England, however, where one example was patented in 1771, and possibly to a greater extent in America during the early nineteenth century. Aaron Burr recorded a circular saw driven by steam in 1806, and between 1810 and 1815 a limited use was accorded this type of saw in America.

In 1817 a notice here declared that *at the steam mill there is a circular saw, about four feet in diameter, chiefly calculated for cutting veneers.* Robert Eastman, of Brunswick, Maine, patented another in 1820. The Massachusetts *Spy*, September 26th, 1821, considered that *The Circular Saw is a recent invention. The Shakers, at their village in Watervliet, near Albany, have this in very excellent use and great perfection.*

A further English notice, in 1831, contained the information that the former use of saws with reciprocating motion had *of late years* been effectually extended by the application of the circular saw, *especially in cutting boards, veneers and every other light description.* Small circular saws were used as early as 1818 in England, to cut nicks in heads of screws.

Appearance of circular kerf marks, on unfinished surfaces of cabinet pieces and seat furniture, has heretofore generally been considered to indicate a date of execution after 1850. While usually true, the preceding notices should indicate the possibility of such marks appearing on examples made between 1820 and 1830, a potentiality which has been definitely proven by experience.

Veneers, which had been cut by hand to one tenth of an inch in thickness during the sixteenth century in southern Europe, and later in France and England, were more economically cut after the introduction of mechanical saws. During the First Empire in France these saws permitted the use of veneers in increasingly thinner and larger sizes. Thirteen to eighteen veneers are said to have then been cut from one-inch mahogany planks.

Introduction of the band saw resulted in cutting evidences, appearing in straight parallel kerf marks which are sharp and set, that always betray modern work. Contrasting to the advances in developing the circular saw, an endless band saw was not perfected until well into the Machine Age. William Newberry, of London, patented one of the early improvisations in 1808, but this proved to be impractical. In 1846 a Mademoiselle Crepin perfected and patented a machine in which a saw belt operated satisfactorily. Other patents followed, including that of Powis & James in 1859.

Of the rough-sawed timbers utilized in furniture-making, various classifications of pines appear more abundantly than any other secondary woods. In America, as in Europe, the terms "spruce," "fir" and "pine" are often synonymous. Opinions concerning the differences in these woods are too often expressed in personal views showing total disregard for those of more authoritative nature, and have been allowed to become instrumental in mislabeling much antique furniture, particularly in America. It may be well, therefore, to consider a summary of information regarding those timbers which may be classed under a broad heading of "pines" in the making of cabinet pieces, slip seat frames, mirror frames and mirror backings.

Fir, with its smooth, silky grain, and color between spruce and pine, was little used outside of the Continent, where it was employed for some construction of furniture and for sound-boards of musical instruments. The term is also loosely used for spruces, especially Norway white spruce, and pines, including the Scots pine.

Spruce, which in America is very hard, often difficult to work and liable to shrink, is also known as "white fir" or "white deal" when emanating from the Baltic regions as a softer wood. There it ranges in quality through various grades used for packing cases, furniture and musical instruments. Baltic spruce shrinks little, is very light in color, with rather straight and even parallel graining, often containing knots with blackish tones or surrounding rings, which alone distinguish some versions from the milder "yellow deal" or "red pine" of the same regions. Norway spruce is noted for exceptional growths in Central Europe.

The pine of southern Europe often resembles Scots pine but is generally softer, while that obtained in northern Europe is largely termed "Danzig fir," and when cut into deals usually displays an even, parallel grain, along with a hard texture. In earlier, as well as present, times it has been specified for architectural and other uses, but seldom supplied, substitution occurring in other Baltic supplies of equal or better quality and with fewer knots.

The Scots pine was transplanted from Norway to Great Britain, and from the seventeenth century to the present day has been imported there as cut timber, together with other pines from Sweden. It has a reddish cast, with distinctive growth rings. The cutting of these timbers by water mills was mentioned by Pepys in 1662-3.

Related northern pines, also known as "fir," "Baltic yellow deal," and "spruce," may emanate from Norway, Sweden, Denmark, Germany or Russia, in red, yellow or white varieties, according to nomenclature, but often less distinctive to the eye.

Alpine pine ranges from the section associated with its name to northern Russia. It is yellowish brown, with a close grain, being light and soft, but shrinking and warping little. Because of its many knots it was procurable only in boards up to about a foot in width, if it was desired with unmarred surfaces.

The northern red pine of America has been classed as Norway pine, and resembles Baltic pine except for a slightly harder grain and redder tone. The texture is moderately coarse but uniform, and the wood has a faint scent and taste of resin. American white or yellow pine is the "Weymouth" pine of Great Britain. It has always been used here with lavish rejection of knotty surfaces. Classed as a soft pine, it has a light straw color, and shrinks little. Technically it has been described as showing identifying very thin, dark, and parallel lines or resin ducts running with the grain, or, with a fine but distinct grain and inconspicuous resin ducts. Cut boards of yellow pine may be found with one side displaying characteristic features, the other resembling pitch pine.

The American southern pine, which has been exported to Europe for many years, looks like Scots pine, but is harder in texture, with a strong pitchy growth. In general, it is one of the most distinctive of the pine timbers, but it is closely similar to, or the same as, pine used in Irish furniture during the eighteenth century.

The most reliable method in accurately determining a species of wood is through examination of cell structures in a cross section with the aid of a lens. However, advice from a leading authority in the identification of timbers by this method has confirmed the belief that even here *it is difficult or impossible to distinguish the woods of closely related species of white pines and yellow pines.*

A further careful regard is expressed by so important an authority as Alexander L. Howard, one of those consulted here, in *Timbers of the World,* 1948, p. 455, under Pine and Fir (with mention of spruce): "The subject is one which is somewhat difficult of comprehension, both on account of the many different sources and consequent variety of the wood itself, and also of the perplexing nomenclature. Names which are in common use in England differ from those on the Continent, and even within the confines of this country they vary according to locality; different names are applied to the same wood; names change with a lapse of time; and finally, names which are botanically quite incorrect are very generally employed, so that these conflicting elements result in continual confusion and dispute."

In view of the preceding opinions, and of practical experiences, it should be reasonably clear that it is often imprudent to base attributions of origin upon the appearance of pinewoods in antique furniture. This is particularly true when such opinions are offered without regard for, or understanding of, the designs represented. Such instances have frequently occurred in this country. American pines (and walnut) have also been returned here in manufactured form, returns which still continue today, and will do so in the future.

In the joining of structural elements, nails gradually came to accompany or replace the wood pegs, or trenails, which had been used from the earliest times. They continued to be produced by hand in many sections after the advent of the Machine Age, and are still obtainable today, newly produced by hand or retrieved from former works. Determination of the use of modern nails, and of brads which generally have their heads punched beneath wood surfaces, is often easily secured by rapping such joined boards sufficiently to expose slight portions of the perfectly round and smooth shanks. Frequently these were insufficiently treated to darken and rust, and consequently reappear in fairly pristine state.

Assemblies made with the use of wood screws may also serve to a degree in determining the appearance of original or later work. Screws were made by hand from the sixteenth century through the latter half of the eighteenth century, when their production became a specialized craft. Later they were partially made by machines, with specially developed tools cutting various thread sizes.

In 1817 the English invented a thread-cutting machine in which the head was *turned* and made ready for the introduction of the nick or cut. Furniture produced from this general period until the middle of the century will sometimes contain original screws in which the revealed heads show some concentric ring marks, differing from those made by modern factory methods. By 1830 factories for making screws had been widely established, and in 1841 reference was made to the fact that "In the infancy of screw-making the thread was formed with a file."

Less sharp and set than the rings of modern screws, the concentric marks produced by these turning machines differ from those appearing on heads of the later products. For some time during the early machine period, wood screws also continued to be made with the bevel and top of the shank cleaned off by a hand file. The top was then filed flat before the nick was cut, thus leaving transverse marks of the file, such as appears on heads of eighteenth century, and earlier, screws.

Attention to the finishing of screw heads may provide a clue when, in examining furniture, it is inconvenient to remove a number of screws for consideration of the threads and blunted ends. If modern concentric ring marks are easily observed, or discoverable after scraping away any concealing wax or other agents, no further time need be lost. However, it should be kept in mind that fairly plentiful supplies of old screws are still available, and that the more skilled fakers of the past have had their supplies made by hand. Some attention has also been paid to filing the heads, as well as the threads, of modern screws to impart an appearance of hand work.

FURNITURE RELATED
TO THE FRENCH SCHOOL

FURNITURE RELATED TO THE FRENCH SCHOOL

1. A Gothic Oak Stool.
   Franco-Flemish, Late XV Century

2. A Gothic Oak Credence Table.
   Dutch, Early XVI Century
   Courtesy of the Rijksmuseum, Amsterdam

A DIRECTORY OF ANTIQUE FURNITURE

3. A GOTHIC WALNUT AND PINE CENTER TABLE. Related examples appearing in Switzerland and Rhenish areas.
South German, XV-XVI Century

4. A LATE GOTHIC OAK CHEST.
Rhenish, XV-XVI Century

FURNITURE RELATED TO THE FRENCH SCHOOL

5. A Henri II Walnut Caqueteuse.
French, XVI Century

6. A Renaissance Walnut
Caqueteuse.   Dutch, XVI Century
Courtesy of the Rijksmuseum, Amsterdam

7. A Walnut Draw-Leaf Table.
Swiss, dated 1598
Courtesy of the Bern Historical Museum, Bern

9. A WALNUT CABINET À DEUX CORPS. School of Cologne, West German, Early XVII Century

FURNITURE RELATED TO THE FRENCH SCHOOL

8. A Walnut Cabinet a Deux Corps.   French, Late XVI Century

10. Upper Portion of an Inlaid Walnut Cabinet à Deux Corps. Displaying Italian and French influences; believed by British authorities to have been executed in England.
Victoria & Albert Museum. Crown Copyright.   School of Cologne, Late XVI Century

A DIRECTORY OF ANTIQUE FURNITURE

11. A Walnut Curule Chair. Related to Italian and German designs.
Dutch, Early XVII Century
Courtesy of the Rijksmuseum, Amsterdam

12. A Carved and Spirally-Turned "Church-Going" Chair.
Dutch, Early XVII Century
Courtesy of the Rijksmuseum, Amsterdam

13. A Walnut Armchair.
Netherlands, XVII Century

14. A Walnut Side Chair. A Dutch form copied in Germany, Scandinavia and England.
Dutch or Scandinavian, XVII Century
Courtesy of the Nordiska Museet, Stockholm

FURNITURE RELATED TO THE FRENCH SCHOOL

15. A Walnut Armchair. With Dutch tapestry covering.
Dutch, XVII Century
Courtesy of the Rijksmuseum, Amsterdam

16. A Walnut Armchair.
Danish, XVII Century
Courtesy of the Dansk Folkemuseum, Copenhagen

17. A Walnut Side Chair. Closely related to French designs.
English, Late XVII Century

18. A Gilded Armchair.
Swedish, Early XVIII Century
Courtesy of the Nordiska Museet, Stockholm

19. A GILDED TORCHERE. In the Louis XIV taste.
Swedish, Early XVIII Century
Courtesy of the Nordiska Museet, Stockholm

20. A WALNUT AND EBONIZED CABINET. West German or Frisian, Early XVIII Century

21. A GILDED WALL MIRROR.
Swedish, Early XVIII Century
Courtesy of the Nordiska Museet, Stockholm

FURNITURE RELATED TO THE FRENCH SCHOOL

22. A LOUIS XIV WALNUT ARMCHAIR. French or West German, circa 1700-1730

23. A WALNUT ARMCHAIR. With elaborate stretcher removed. South German, XVIII Century

26. AN ARMCHAIR OF LIEGE DESIGN. With Spanish carving. Hispano-Flemish, XVIII Century

27. A GILDED ARMCHAIR. With period needlepoint covering. Described as "Georgian." West German, XVIII Century

24. A Gilded State Chair. Made for the Stadholder of the Admiralty.
Amsterdam, 1748
Courtesy of the Rijksmuseum, Amsterdam

25. A Gilded State Chair.
Venetian, XVIII Century

28. A Régence Walnut Fauteuil.
Dutch, XVIII Century

29. A Walnut Armchair.
Genoese, XVIII Century

30. A Walnut Canapé.
Swiss or Piedmontese, XVIII Century

12 A DIRECTORY OF ANTIQUE FURNITURE

31. A GILDED CONSOLE TABLE.
Italian or South German,
Early XVIII Century

32. A GILDED CENTER TABLE.
Dutch, Early XVIII Century
Courtesy of the Rijksmuseum, Amsterdam

33. AN AMARANTH PARQUETRY COMMODE. The *bronze doré* mounts formerly attributed to Cressent.
German, XVIII Century
Photograph by Taylor & Dull

34. A Kingwood Parquetry Commode. Expertized as a French Régence example. South German, XVIII Century

FURNITURE RELATED TO THE FRENCH SCHOOL

37. A GILDED PIER MIRROR. With blue glass border. Described as English work of the late seventeenth century.
German, XVIII Century

35. A PAINTED AND GILDED COMMODE.
South German, XVIII Century

36. A GILDED WOOD AND GESSOR PIER MIRROR.
　　Dutch, Early XVIII Century

38. A GILDED PIER MIRROR. With etched glass border.
　　Swedish, XVIII Century
Courtesy of the Nordiska Museet, Stockholm

39. A GILDED WALL MIRROR.
　　North Italian, Early XVIII Century

40. AN ALL-GLASS PIER MIRROR. With etched border and surrounds.
　　Swedish, XVIII Century
Courtesy of the Nordiska Museet, Stockholm

FURNITURE RELATED TO THE FRENCH SCHOOL

41. A Louis XV Gilded Fauteuil.
Swedish, XVIII Century
Courtesy of the Nordiska Museet, Stockholm

42. A Louis XV Painted and Gilded Fauteuil. Venetian, XVIII Century

43. A Louis XV Painted Fauteuil.
Swedish, XVIII Century
Courtesy of the Nordiska Museet, Stockholm

44. A Louis XV Carved Ash Side Chair.
West German, XVIII Century

45. A Louis XV Painted Side Chair.
North Italian, XVIII Century

46. A Louis XV Painted Side Chair.
Swedish, XVIII Century
Courtesy of the Nordiska Museet, Stockholm

48. A Louis XV Painted and Gilded Fauteuil.   German, XVIII Century

47. A Louis XV Painted and Gilded Fauteuil.   German, XVIII Century

FURNITURE RELATED TO THE FRENCH SCHOOL

50. A LOUIS XV PAINTED AND GILDED
SIDE CHAIR. German, XVIII Century

51. A LOUIS XV PAINTED FAUTEUIL.
Swedish, XVIII Century

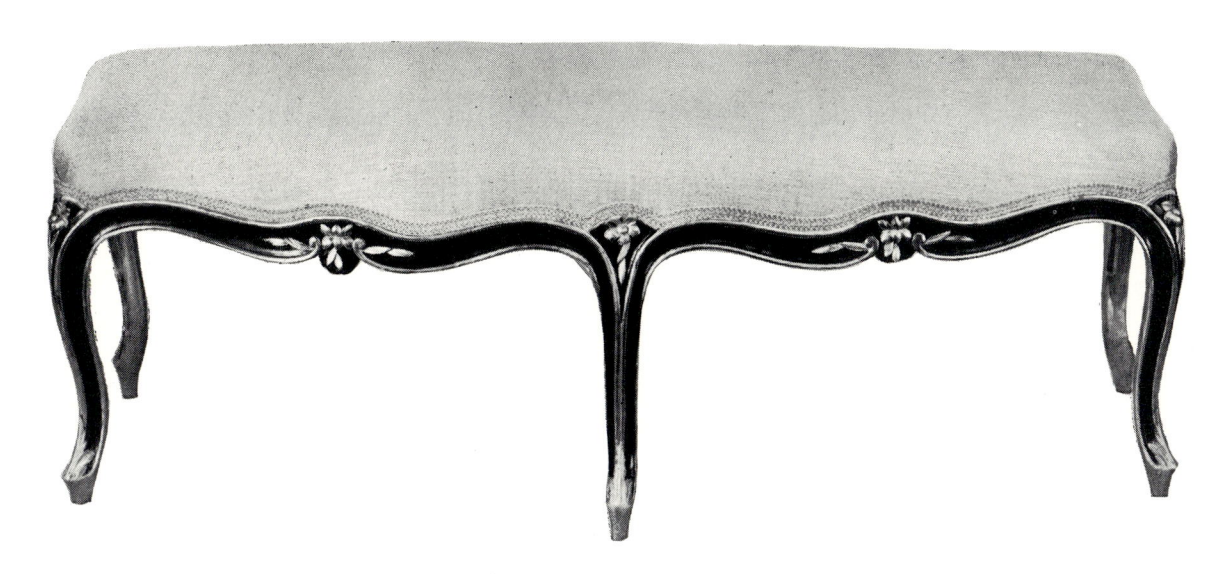

49. A LOUIS XV PAINTED AND GILDED BANQUETTE. Recently published as "French Provincial."
German, XVIII Century

52. A LOUIS XV PAINTED FAUTEUIL. With apocryphal stamp of Jean-Baptiste Fromogeau, a French *ébéniste* noted for his superior cabinetwork.
Scandinavian, XVIII Century

53. A LOUIS XV PAINTED AND GILDED BERGERE. With original leather covering. Swedish, XVIII Century
Courtesy of the Nordiska Museet, Stockholm

54. A GILDED AND DECORATED BLACK LACQUER CENTER TABLE.
German, XVIII Century

FURNITURE RELATED TO THE FRENCH SCHOOL

55. A Louis XV Kingwood Gaming Table. Inlaid with oyster parquetry.
Genoese, XVIII Century

56. A Louis XV-XVI Sycamore Marquetry Poudreuse.
David Roentgen,
Neuwied, circa 1775

A DIRECTORY OF ANTIQUE FURNITURE

57. An Olivewood and Kingwood Gaming and Writing Table.
German, XVIII Century

58. A Louis XV Kingwood Bureau Plat.   Italian or South German, XVIII Century

FURNITURE RELATED TO THE FRENCH SCHOOL

59. A Painted and Gilded Console Table. Related to Piedmontese designs. South German, XVIII Century

61. A Louis XV Gilded Console Table. German or Danish, XVIII Century

60. A Louis XV Gilded Console Table. Described as English! German, XVIII Century

24 A DIRECTORY OF ANTIQUE FURNITURE

62. A LOUIS XV KINGWOOD COMMODE. Inlaid with characteristic triangulate parquetry panels.
Swedish, XVIII Century
Courtesy of the Nordiska Museet, Stockholm

63. A LOUIS XV KINGWOOD COMMODE. Inlaid with diamond parquetry; the escutcheons designed as mascarons with open-mouth apertures. Swedish, XVIII Century
Courtesy of the Nordiska Museet, Stockholm

FURNITURE RELATED TO THE FRENCH SCHOOL

64. A Louis XV Commode. Inlaid with a characteristic parquetry design. Genoese, XVIII Century

65. A Louis XV Amaranth and Citronnier Commode. German, XVIII Century

66. A LOUIS XV BOMBÉ-FRONT COMMODE. Inlaid with blocked chevron parquetry.
Dutch, XVIII Century
Courtesy of the Rijksmuseum, Amsterdam

67. A LOUIS XV COMMODE. Inlaid with triangulate parquetry panels.
Swedish, XVIII Century
Courtesy of the Dansk Folkemuseum, Copenhagen

FURNITURE RELATED TO THE FRENCH SCHOOL

68. A LOUIS XV KINGWOOD COMMODE. The diamond parquetry and *bronze doré* work related to Swedish developments.
Potsdam or Berlin, XVIII Century

69. A LOUIS XV KINGWOOD COMMODE.
German, XVIII Century

71. A Louis XV Carved Oak Commode.   Liege, XVIII Century

72. A Louis XV Walnut Commode. North Italian, XVIII Century

FURNITURE RELATED TO THE FRENCH SCHOOL

73. A Louis XV-XVI Painted and Gilded Encoignure.
German, XVIII Century

70. A Louis XV Carved Oak Commode. Liege, XVIII Century

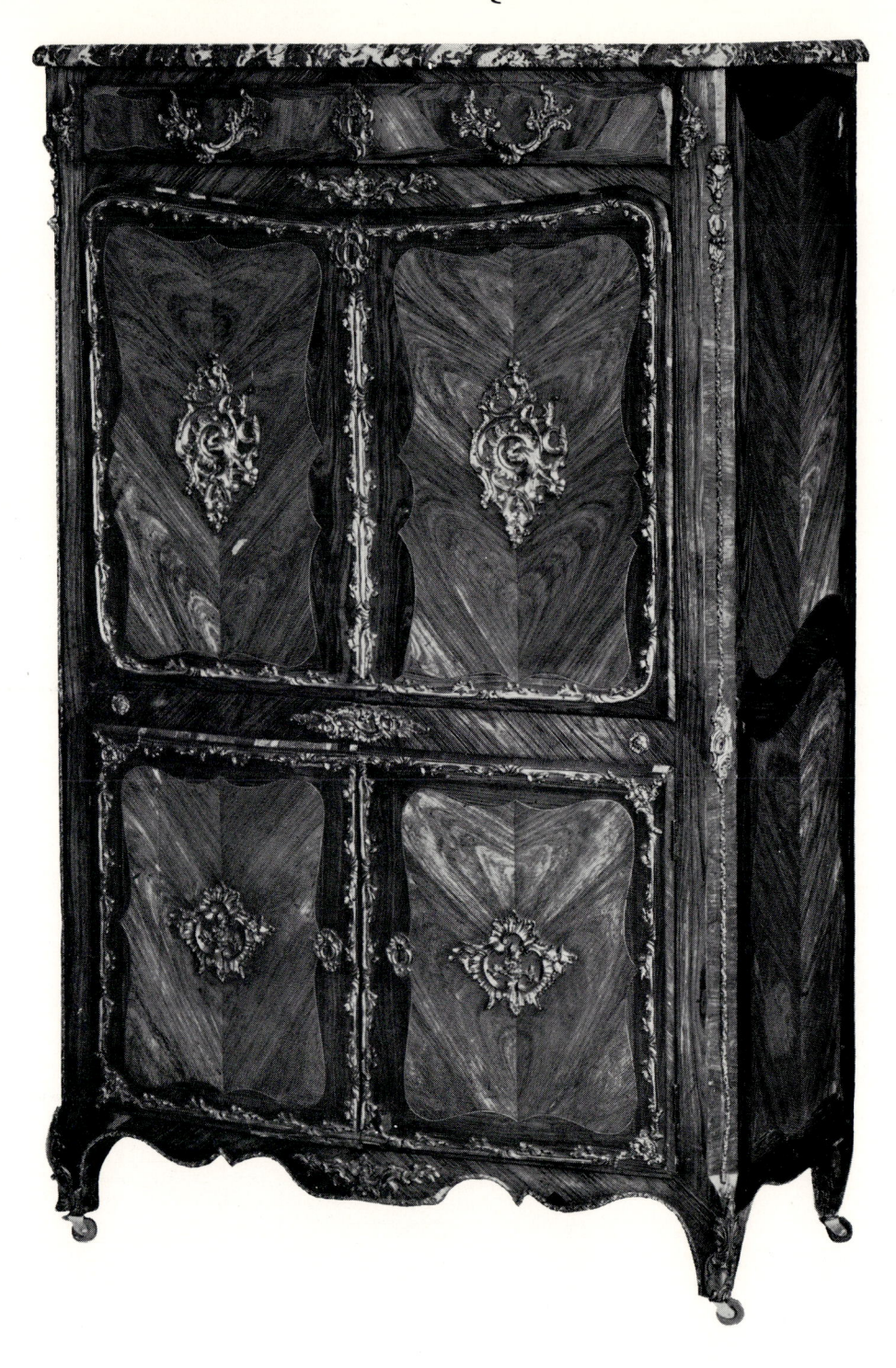

74. A Louis XV Kingwood Secrétaire à Abattant.   German, XVIII Century

FURNITURE RELATED TO THE FRENCH SCHOOL

77. A Gilded Pier Mirror. Dutch, XVIII Century

76. A Louis XV Gilded Pier Mirror. South German, XVIII Century

75. A Louis XV Gilded Pier Mirror. With plate border. Swedish, XVIII Century

80. A Louis XV Gilded Wall Mirror. Representing a type of work carried out by Italian carvers throughout Europe. Italian, XVIII Century

79. A Gilded Wall Mirror. North Italian, XVIII Century

78. A Gilded Wall Mirror. German, XVIII Century

FURNITURE RELATED TO THE FRENCH SCHOOL

82. A Louis XV Bronze Doré Cartel. Berlin, XVIII Century

83. A Louis XV-XVI Bronze Doré Cartel. Roentgen and Kinzing, Neuwied, XVIII Century

81. A Louis XV Bronze Doré Cartel. Viennese, XVIII Century

84. A LOUIS XVI PAINTED VOYEUSE.
Swedish, XVIII Century
Courtesy of the Nordiska Museet, Stockholm

85. A LOUIS XVI GILDED SIDE CHAIR.
Swedish, XVIII Century
Courtesy of the Nordiska Museet, Stockholm

86. A LOUIS XVI WALNUT FAUTEUIL.
Dutch, XVIII Century
Courtesy of the Rijksmuseum, Amsterdam

87. A LOUIS XVI PAINTED FAUTEUIL.
German, XVIII Century

FURNITURE RELATED TO THE FRENCH SCHOOL

88. A Louis XVI Painted Fauteuil.
Dutch, XVIII Century
Courtesy of the Rijksmuseum, Amsterdam

89. A Louis XVI Painted Side Chair.
Dutch, XVIII Century

90. A Louis XVI Painted Fauteuil.
Swedish, XVIII Century
Courtesy of the Nordiska Museet, Stockholm

91. A Louis XVI Painted Fauteuil De Bureau.
Swedish, XVIII Century
Courtesy of the Nordiska Museet, Stockholm

92. A LOUIS XVI GILDED FAUTEUIL. With Russian tapestry covering.
Russian, XVIII Century

94. A LOUIS XVI FAUTEUIL. Described as a pine armchair of the Adam period.
West German, XVIII Century

93. A LOUIS XVI PAINTED AND GILDED FAUTEUIL. Formerly described as English work of the Adam period.
German, XVIII Century

95. A LOUIS XVI GILDED CANAPÉ.
Swedish, XVIII Century
Courtesy of the Nordiska Museet, Stockholm

FURNITURE RELATED TO THE FRENCH SCHOOL

96. A Louis XVI Painted Canapé.   Swedish, XVIII Century
Courtesy of the Nordiska Museet, Stockholm

97. A Louis XVI Gilded Canapé. Displaying the influence of Georges Jacob.
Potsdam, Late XVIII Century

98. A Louis XVI Painted Écran.
Dutch, XVIII Century
Courtesy of the Rijksmuseum, Amsterdam

99. A Louis XVI Walnut Parquetry Center Table. West German or Alsatian, XVIII Century

100. A Louis XVI Table à Écrire.
Georg Haupt, Stockholm,
circa 1780
Courtesy of the Nordiska Museet, Stockholm

101. An Inlaid Sycamore Center Table. With embroidery panel.
German, XVIII Century

FURNITURE RELATED TO THE FRENCH SCHOOL

102. A LOUIS XVI PARQUETRY POUDREUSE. The top surfaces inlaid with marquetry floral ornament.
Swedish, XVIII Century
Courtesy of the Nordiska Museet, Stockholm

103. A LOUIS XVI MARQUETRY BUREAU À PENTE. Related inlays of writing implements occasionally appear in English furniture.
Swedish, XVIII Century
Courtesy of the Nordiska Museet, Stockholm

104. A LOUIS XVI MARQUETRY SECRÉTAIRE À ABATTANT.
Georg Haupt, Stockholm, circa 1780
Courtesy of the Nordiska Museet, Stockholm

105. A Louis XVI Gilded Console.
Swedish, XVIII Century
Courtesy of the Nordiska Museet, Stockholm

106. A Louis XVI Painted Console Table. Dutch, XVIII Century
Courtesy of the Rijksmuseum, Amsterdam

FURNITURE RELATED TO THE FRENCH SCHOOL

107. A Louis XVI Marquetry Commode. Georg Haupt, Stockholm, 1779
Courtesy of the Nordiska Museet, Stockholm

108. A Louis XVI Kingwood and Tulipwood Commode. With typical Dutch handles and escutcheons. Rhenish, XVIII Century

A DIRECTORY OF ANTIQUE FURNITURE

109. A Louis XVI Marquetry Commode. Flemish or West German, XVIII Century
Courtesy of the Rijksmuseum, Amsterdam

110. A Louis XVI Acajou Commode. Leipzig, Late XVIII Century

FURNITURE RELATED TO THE FRENCH SCHOOL

112. A Louis XVI Painted and
Decorated Commode.
Swedish, Late XVIII Century
Courtesy of the Nordiska Museet, Stockholm

111. A Louis XVI Walnut Commode. South German, XVIII Century

A DIRECTORY OF ANTIQUE FURNITURE

114. A Louis XVI Burl Birch Table à Gradin. The legs fitted with threaded silver-metal cappings, enabling removal for distant deliveries. From the Strogonoff Collection, Leningrad.
David Roentgen,
Neuwied, circa 1785-1790

115. A Louis XVI Acajou Bureau à Cylindre.
North German, XVIII Century

113. A Louis XVI Sycamore Marquetry Bureau à Cylindre. The center drawer inlaid with "DR" monogram. David Roentgen, Neuwied, circa 1780

117. A SYCAMORE AND SATINWOOD CABINET. With mother-of-pearl ornament in lacquer panels.
Dutch, Late XVIII Century

116. A LOUIS XVI MARQUETRY SECRÉTAIRE À ABATTANT.
Gottlieb Iwersson, Stockholm, 1781
Courtesy of the Nordiska Museet, Stockholm

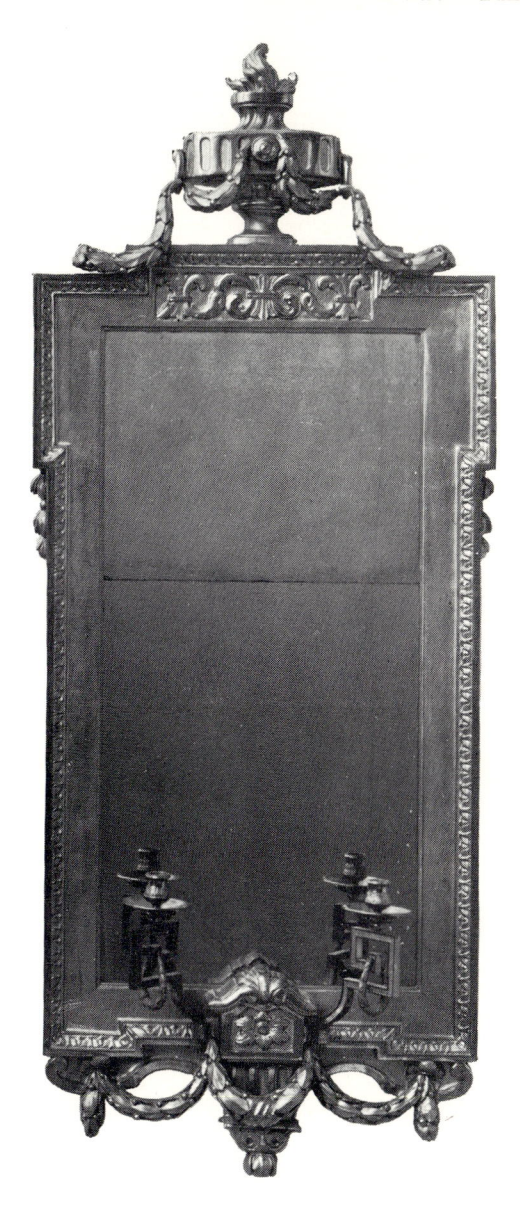

FURNITURE RELATED TO THE FRENCH SCHOOL

122. A Louis XVI Carved, Painted and Gilded Appliqué.
Swedish, XVIII Century
Courtesy of the Rohsska Konstslojdmuseet, Goteborg

118. A Louis XVI Gilded Girandole Mirror. Swedish, XVIII Century
Courtesy of the Nordiska Museet, Stockholm

121. A Louis XVI Bronze Doré Cartel. Stockholm, XVIII Century
Courtesy of the Nordiska Museet, Stockholm

119. A LOUIS XVI GILDED PIER MIRROR. Closely related to Italian and French designs. German or Danish, Late XVIII Century

120. A LOUIS XVI GILDED WALL MIRROR. Described as a Southern French or Italian example. North German, XVIII Century

FURNITURE RELATED TO THE FRENCH SCHOOL

123. A Directoire Acajou Side Chair.
North German, Late XVIII Century

124. A Directoire Painted and Gilded Fauteuil. The laurel-sheathed legs, especially, related to carved work in furniture made for Harewood House.
North Italian, Late XVIII Century

125. A Directoire Painted Side Chair. Stockholm, circa 1800
Courtesy of the Nordiska Museet, Stockholm

126. A Directoire Painted and Decorated Side Chair.
Florentine, circa 1810

A DIRECTORY OF ANTIQUE FURNITURE

130. A Directoire Gilded Tripod Stand. In the Pompeian style. Related to French designs, such as the famous pair of console tables in the Palais de Fontainbleau; and to those of Thomas Hope. Swedish, circa 1800
Courtesy of the Nordiska Museet, Stockholm

127. A Satinwood Tea Comfort.
Dutch, circa 1810

128. A Satinwood Tea Comfort.
Dutch, circa 1810

129. A Directoire Acajou Torchere.
West German or Dutch, circa 1800

FURNITURE RELATED TO THE FRENCH SCHOOL

131. A Directoire Yewwood Table
à Écrire.   Viennese, circa 1800

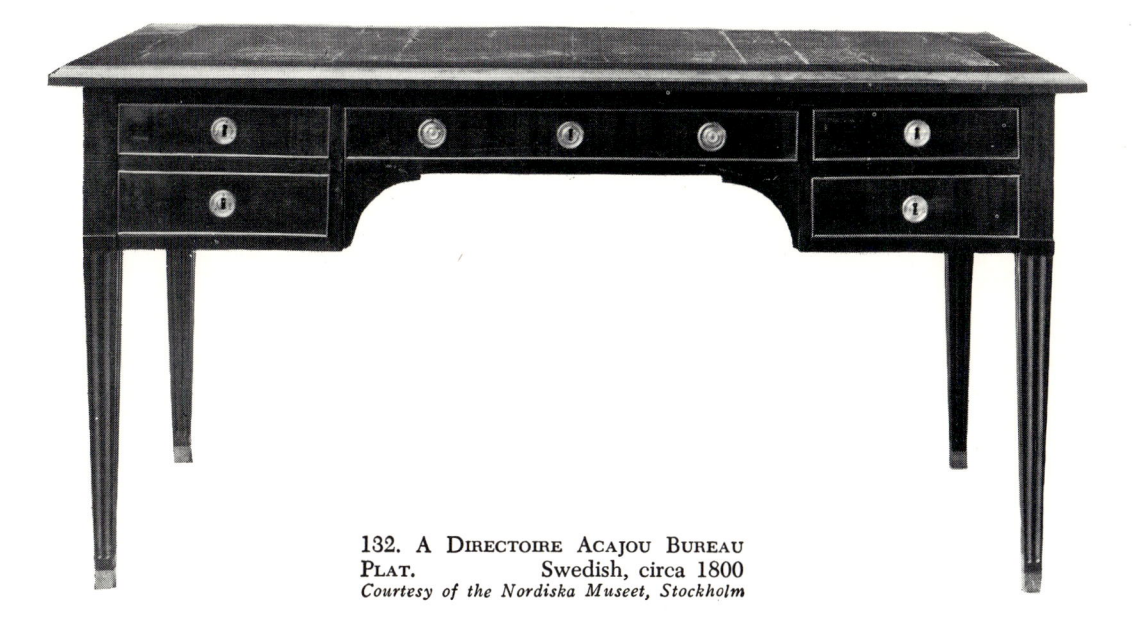

132. A Directoire Acajou Bureau
Plat.   Swedish, circa 1800
Courtesy of the Nordiska Museet, Stockholm

133. A Directoire Acajou Console Table. German, circa 1800

134. A Directoire Mahogany Card Table. By a craftsman whose designs remained alien to those of his adopted country; present-day reaction refutes this choice. Honoré Lannuier, New York City, circa 1810

135. A Directoire Acajou Card Table. With poplar-lined end drawers, and square-toothed gate hinges, as in American practice.
North German, circa 1800

136. A Directoire Gilded Console. Viennese or South German, circa 1800

FURNITURE RELATED TO THE FRENCH SCHOOL

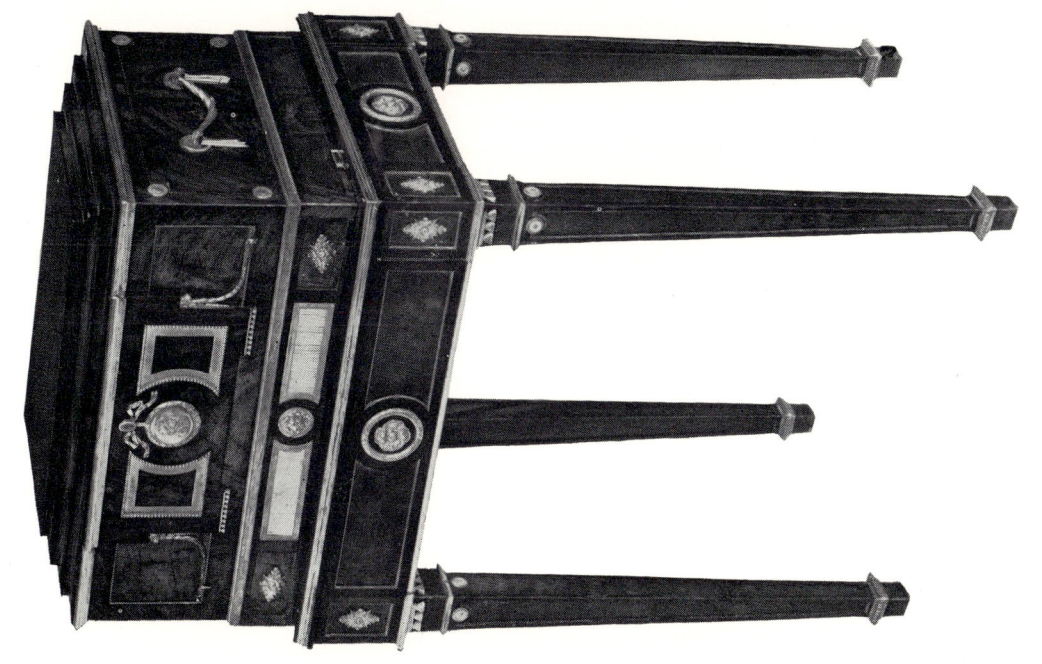

137. A DIRECTOIRE ACAJOU COFFRET. With original stand. Ingenious mechanical contrivances operated by turns of a single key in two concealed apertures. The design copied in Sweden. David Roentgen, Neuwied, circa 1790

140. A DIRECTOIRE ACAJOU COMMODE. Erik Nystrom, Stockholm, circa 1790
Courtesy of the Nordiska Museet, Stockholm

139. A Directoire Elm and Birch Commode. Swedish, circa 1800
Courtesy of the Nordiska Museet, Stockholm

138. A Directoire Citronnier Commode. German, circa 1800

FURNITURE RELATED TO THE FRENCH SCHOOL

142. A Directoire Acajou Bureau à Cylindre. German, circa 1795

141. A Directoire Acajou Bureau à Cylindre. School of David Roentgen. North German, circa 1790
Courtesy of the Museum für Kunst und Gewerbe, Hamburg

56 A DIRECTORY OF ANTIQUE FURNITURE

143. A Directoire Acajou Secrétaire à Abattant. The colonettes associated in America with "Bilbao" mirrors. Swedish, circa 1810
144. A Directoire Acajou and Merisier Secrétaire à Abattant. North German, circa 1800

FURNITURE RELATED TO THE FRENCH SCHOOL

147. A DIRECTOIRE GILDED CARTEL.
With *eglomisé* panels.
Stockholm, circa 1800
Courtesy of the Nordiska Museet, Stockholm

148. A DIRECTOIRE GILDED CARTEL.
Stockholm, circa 1800
Courtesy of the Nordiska Museet, Stockholm

145. A DIRECTOIRE PARCEL-GILDED MAHOGANY PIER MIRROR. With characteristics of Berlin and Potsdam designs.
German, circa 1795

146. A DIRECTOIRE PARCEL-GILDED CHERRYWOOD WALL MIRROR. The carved details similar to those appearing in architectural designs of Berlin and Potsdam. German, circa 1795

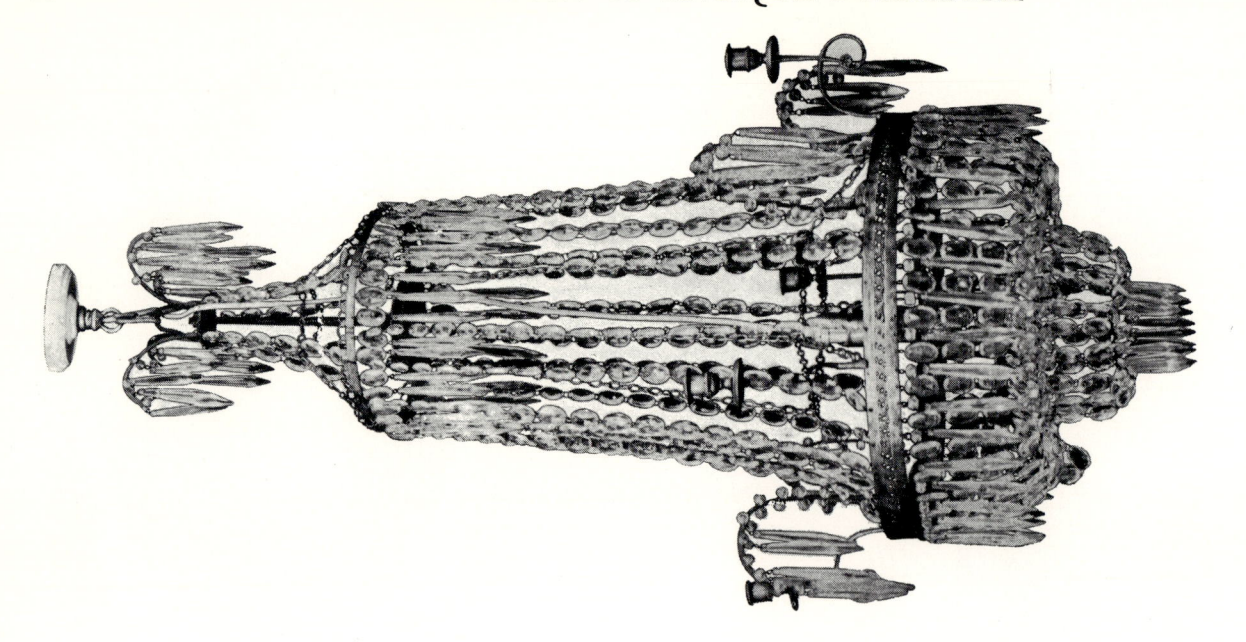

58   A DIRECTORY OF ANTIQUE FURNITURE

149. A Directoire Cut Glass and Ormolu Chandeliere.
German, circa 1800

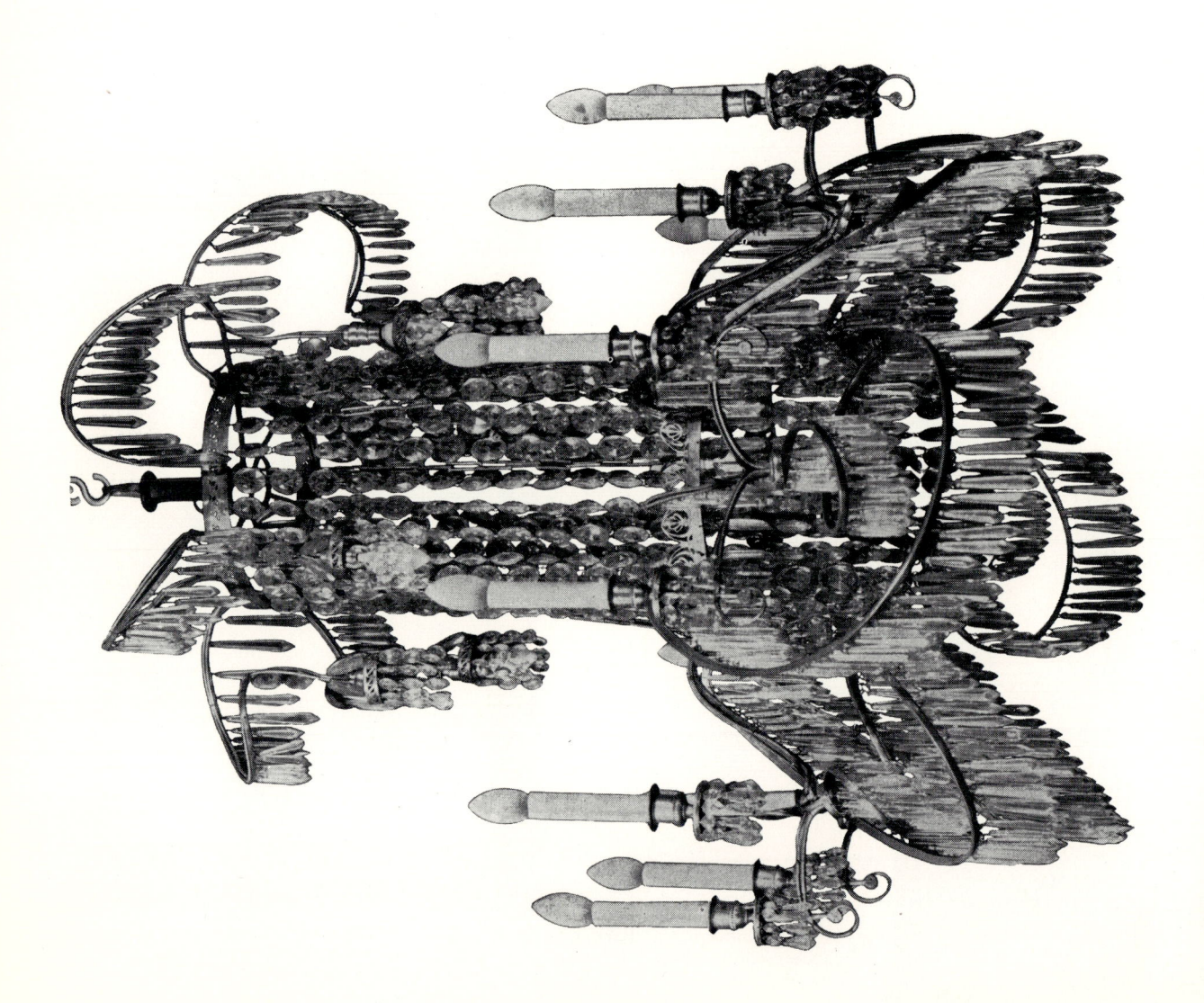

150. A Directoire Cut Glass and Ormolu Chandeliere.
German, circa 1800

FURNITURE RELATED TO THE FRENCH SCHOOL

151. AN EMPIRE PAINTED AND GILDED SIDE CHAIR. More related designs of this type appear in Germany than in Italy.
Italian or South German, circa 1810

152. AN EMPIRE PAINTED AND GILDED ARMCHAIR. Italian, circa 1810

153. AN EMPIRE FRUITWOOD ARMCHAIR. Austrian, circa 1815

157. AN EMPIRE PARCEL-GILDED MAHOGANY CARD TABLE. Style of Honoré Lannuier. The ormolu mounts apparently made in Great Britain.
New York City, circa 1815

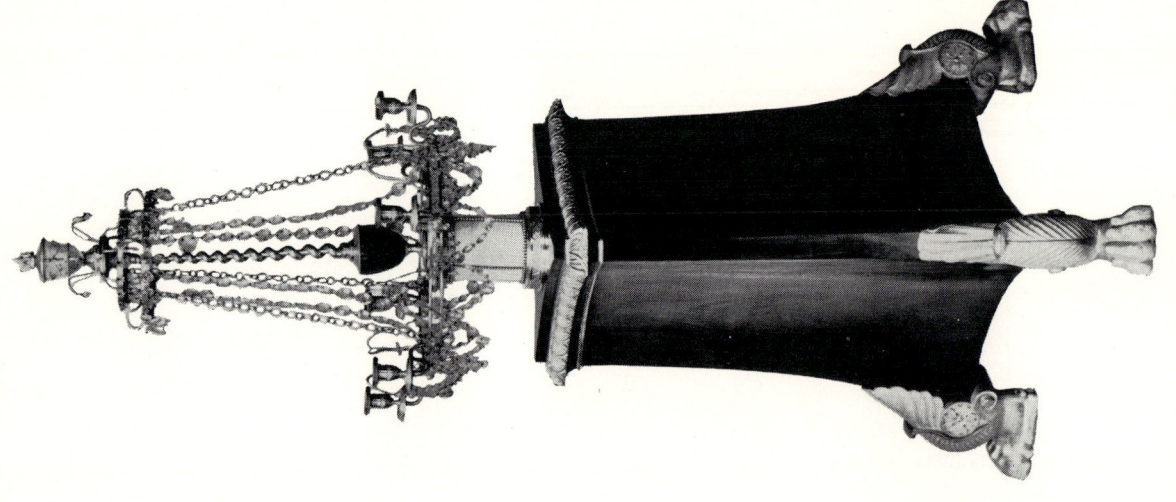

156. An Empire Glass and Ormolu Candelabrum with Mahogany Pedestal. Stockholm, circa 1810
Courtesy of the Nordiska Museet, Stockholm

154. An Empire Citronnier Gueridon. Viennese or South German, circa 1810

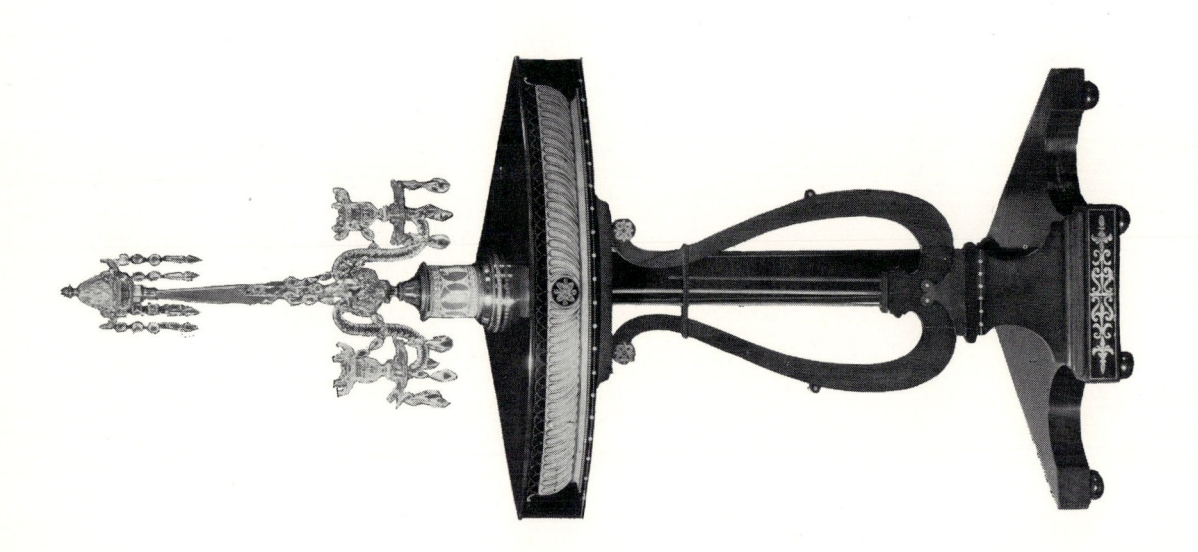

155. A "Regency Inlaid Mahogany Corner Console." Described as English work; the principal material apparently cherrywood. Viennese or German, circa 1810

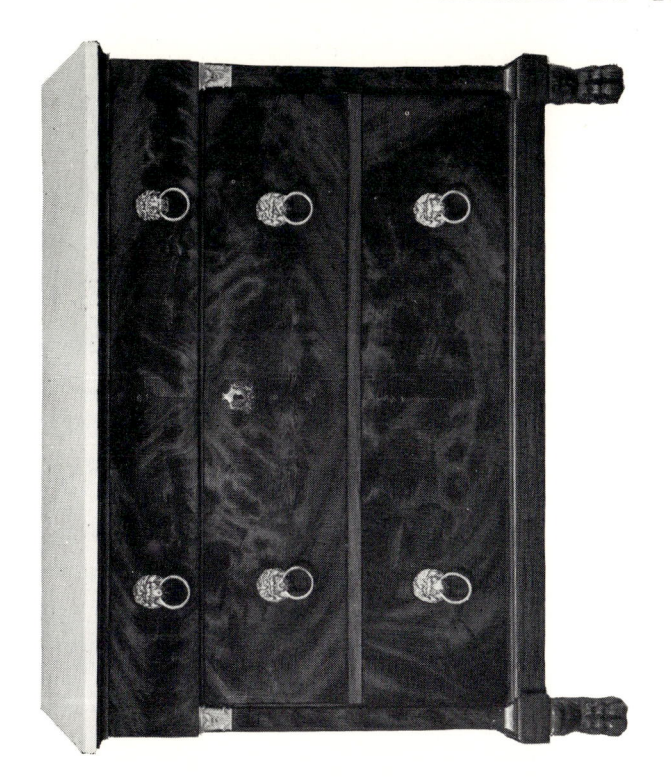

FURNITURE RELATED TO THE FRENCH SCHOOL

158. AN EMPIRE MAHOGANY COMMODE. Combining American structural techniques with an alien design.
Honoré Lannuier,
New York City, circa 1815

159. AN EMPIRE MAHOGANY SECRÉTAIRE À ABATTANT. Recently published as "French Provincial." Possibly of Munich origin.
German, circa 1815

FURNITURE RELATED
TO THE ENGLISH SCHOOL

A DIRECTORY OF ANTIQUE FURNITURE

160. A Walnut Armchair.
Dutch, XVII Century

161. A Walnut Armchair.
Dutch, XVII Century

162. A Walnut Armchair.
Flemish, XVII Century

163. A Walnut Side Chair. With monogram of Karl XII. The "slice" scrolls were also favored in England and Germany.
Swedish, XVII-XVIII Century
Courtesy of the Nordiska Museet, Stockholm

FURNITURE RELATED TO THE ENGLISH SCHOOL

164. A Walnut Side Chair.
Dutch, circa 1700

165. A Walnut Side Chair.
Rhenish, circa 1700

166. A Walnut Side Chair.
Dutch or West German, circa 1700

167. A Walnut Side Chair.
Dutch, circa 1700

A DIRECTORY OF ANTIQUE FURNITURE

168. A Walnut Side Chair.
Dutch, circa 1720

169. A Walnut Side Chair.
Dutch, circa 1720

170. A Walnut Side Chair.
Dutch, circa 1720

171. A Walnut and Pine Side Chair.
With embroidery panels.
Scandinavian, Early XVIII Century

172. A Walnut and Needlepoint Cheval Screen.
Dutch, Early XVIII Century

174. A Painted and Gilded Console Table. Dutch, Early XVII Century
Courtesy of the Rijksmuseum, Amsterdam

173. An Oak Draw-Leaf Table.
Flemish or West German,
Early XVII Century

175. A Walnut Oysterwood Parquetry Center Table.
Dutch, Late XVII Century

176. An Ebony Marquetry Coffret on Stand. Danish or North German, Early XVIII Century
Courtesy of the Nordiska Museet, Stockholm

FURNITURE RELATED TO THE ENGLISH SCHOOL

177. A WALNUT CABINET ON STAND.
North German, Early XVIII Century
Courtesy of the Dansk Folkemuseum, Copenhagen

178. A WALNUT CABINET. Inlaid with oyster panels and marquetry.
North German, Early XVIII Century
Courtesy of the Dansk Folkemuseum, Copenhagen

179. A Maple Buttwood Cabinet on Stand. Inlaid with brass stringing lines, and marquetry.
German, Early XVIII Century

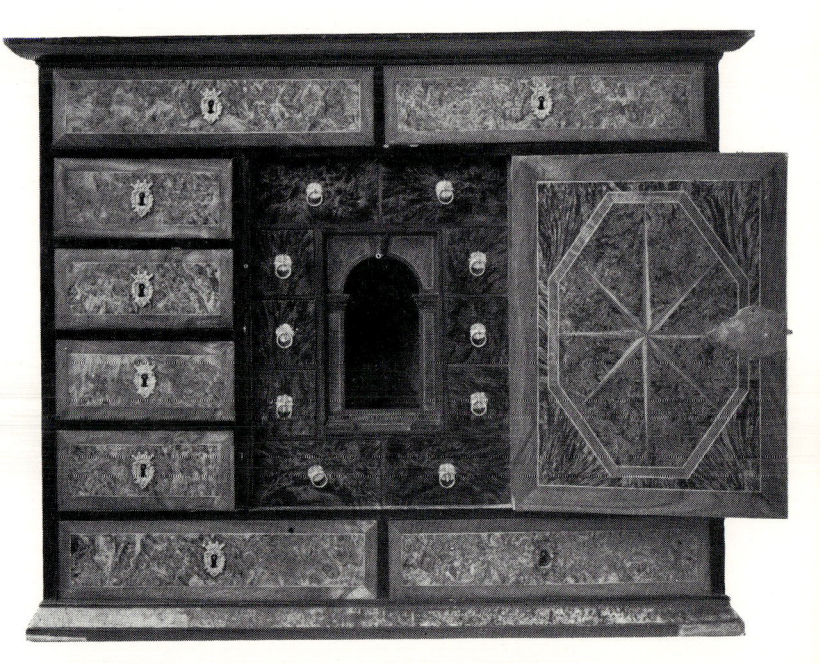

180. Upper Stage of a Burlwood Cabinet. Similar crowned escutcheons appear on English furniture.
Swedish, Early XVIII Century
Courtesy of the Nordiska Museet, Stockholm

FURNITURE RELATED TO THE ENGLISH SCHOOL

181. A WALNUT WALL MIRROR.
Swedish, Early XVIII Century
Courtesy of the Nordiska Museet, Stockholm

182. A WALNUT WALL MIRROR.
Scandinavian, Early XVIII Century

70 A DIRECTORY OF ANTIQUE FURNITURE

183. A Queen Anne Walnut Side Chair.
Swedish, Early XVIII Century
Courtesy of the Nordiska Museet, Stockholm

184. A Maple or Beech Armchair.
Schleswig Holstein, XVIII Century

187. A Walnut Side Chair.
Dutch, XVIII Century

185. A Maple Armchair. The splat with no separate shoepiece.
North German or Danish, XVIII Century

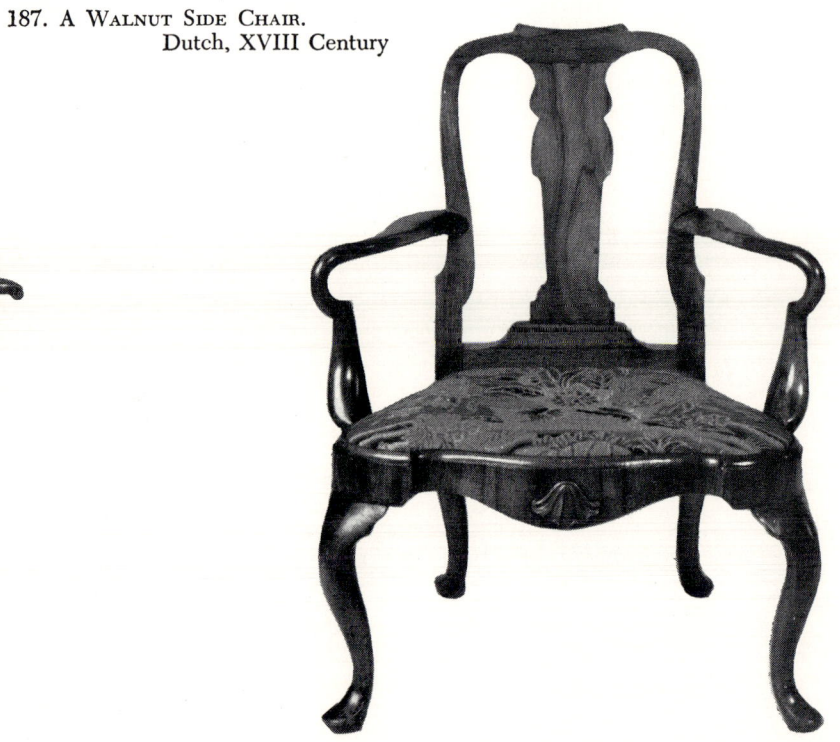

186. A Walnut Armchair.
North German, XVIII Century

FURNITURE RELATED TO THE ENGLISH SCHOOL

188. A Walnut Marquetry Armchair. Dutch, XVIII Century

190. A Walnut Armchair. North German, XVIII Century

191. A Cherrywood Side Chair. A Hanse town example, probably of Danzig origin, with front and rear feet of Irish types.
North German, XVIII Century

192. A Late Baroque Wing Chair. Swedish, XVIII Century
Courtesy of the Nordiska Museet, Stockholm

189. A Walnut and Beech Side Chair. Dutch, XVIII Century

193. An Inlaid Walnut Card Table. Of Dutch type, the top opening to dished pockets.
North German, XVIII Century

195. A Walnut Side Table.
Dutch, XVIII Century

194. A Cherrywood Card Table.
Dutch or North German,
XVIII Century

FURNITURE RELATED TO THE ENGLISH SCHOOL

196. A Black and Gold Lacquer Cabinet. With typical cresting.
Dutch, Early XVIII Century

198. A Walnut Secretary. The feet, mirror panels and hardware are replacements.
Dutch, Early XVIII Century

197. A Decorated Lacquer Secretary. "The shutters of palisander or other related wood of the Dutch East Indies . . . oak and white *pine* in the carcase." The finials, interior corbels, etc., of Dutch rather than English design. Dutch School, Early XVIII Century
Courtesy of the Kunsthistorisch Instituut, Leuven, Belgium

FURNITURE RELATED TO THE ENGLISH SCHOOL

201. AN IMPORTANT WALNUT SECRETARY. With mirrored pilasters. Exhibited as a Treasure of English Art. One of a pair.
Saxony, circa 1730-1740

202. A Walnut Secretary.
Danish, Early XVIII Century

199. A Walnut Chest of Drawers.
Dutch, XVIII Century

200. A Burl Walnut Secretary.
Dutch, XVIII Century
Courtesy of the Rijksmuseum, Amsterdam

FURNITURE RELATED TO THE ENGLISH SCHOOL

204. A MARQUETRY FALL-FRONT WRITING CABINET. Believed to be of Dutch origin. The appearance of pine, and the marquetry decoration suggest Danish or North German work. Probably Danish, circa 1700
Victoria & Albert Museum, Crown Copyright.

203. A WALNUT AND BURLWOOD CABINET. With patchwork veneers. Schleswig Holstein, Early XVIII Century

206. A Walnut and Indian Wood Cabinet.
Dutch, Early XVIII Century
Courtesy of the Rijksmuseum, Amsterdam

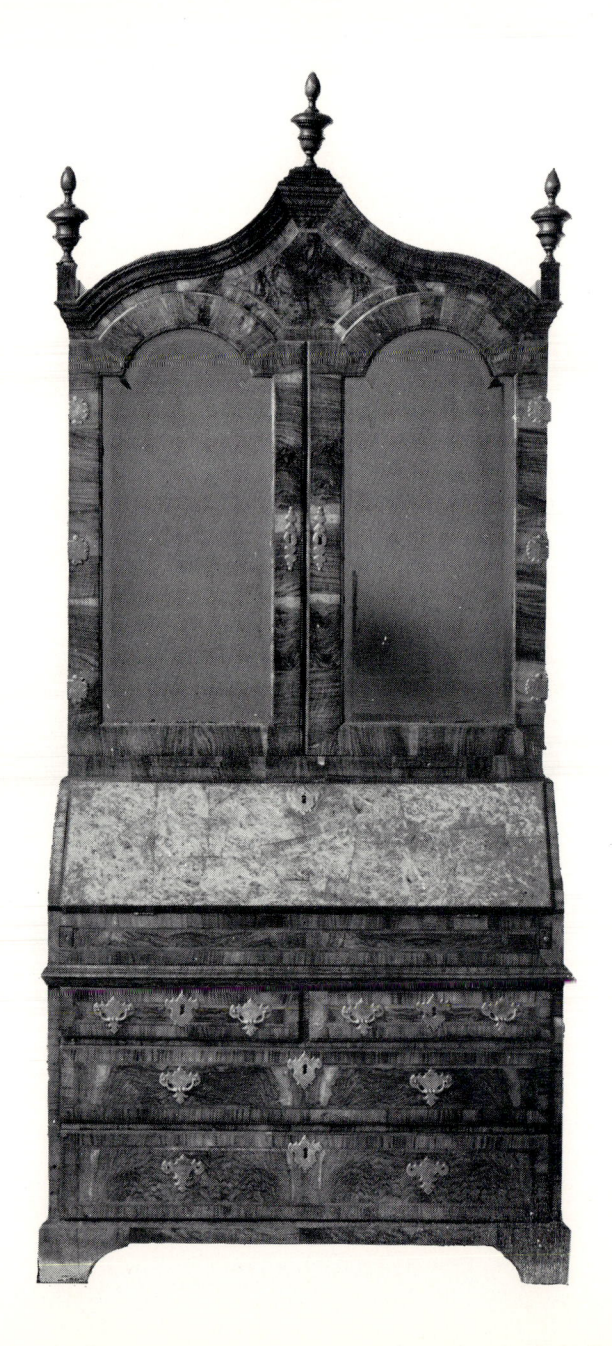

208. A Walnut and Burlwood Secretary. The slant lid faced with patchwork veneers.
North German or a neighboring state, XVIII Century
Courtesy of the Nordiska Museet, Stockholm

205. A Burl Ash Secretary.   Dutch, Early XVIII Century

207. A Burl Walnut Secretary.
Dutch, XVIII Century

209. A Walnut Secretary. The applied mask possibly of varying origin.
Schleswig Holstein, XVIII Century

FURNITURE RELATED TO THE ENGLISH SCHOOL

210. A Gilded Pier Mirror.
Dutch, Early XVIII Century

211. A Decorated Red Lacquer Pier Mirror. Closely following Dutch examples. Swedish, Early XVIII Century
Courtesy of the Rohsska Konstslojdmuseet, Goteborg

212. A Parcel-Gilded Walnut Pier Mirror.   Danish, XVIII Century

213. A Parcel-Gilded Walnut Pier Mirror.   North German or Danish, XVIII Century

216. A Walnut Wall Mirror.
Danish, XVIII Century

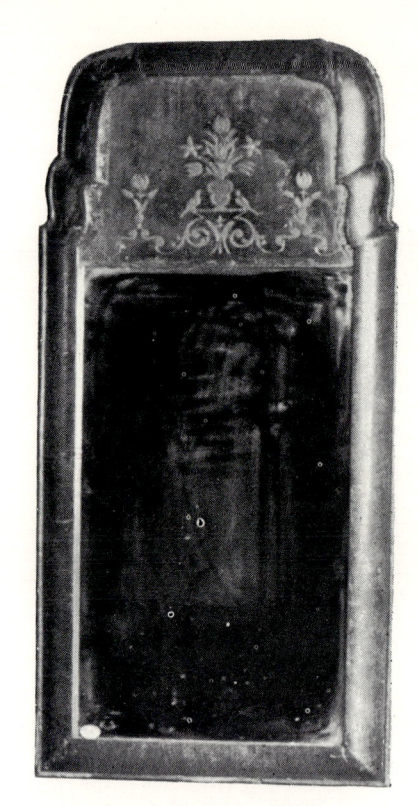

215. A Walnut Wall Mirror. The upper plate with etched design.
Danish, XVIII Century

214. A Walnut Pier Mirror.
Danish, XVIII Century

217. A Parcel-Gilded Walnut Wall Mirror. Danish or North German, XVIII Century

FURNITURE RELATED TO THE ENGLISH SCHOOL

218. A BEECH ARMCHAIR. Exhibited as American.
North German, XVIII Century

219. A WALNUT SIDE CHAIR.
North German, XVIII Century

220. A WALNUT SIDE CHAIR.
Dutch, XVIII Century

222. A WALNUT AND BEECH SIDE CHAIR.   Danzig, XVIII Century

221. A "QUEEN ANNE MAPLE SIDE CHAIR."   Swedish or Norwegian, XVIII Century

A DIRECTORY OF ANTIQUE FURNITURE

225. A Mahogany Side Chair. Regarded as a native example by authority in Holland; the design was adopted in Denmark, Germany and Ireland, with local variations.
Dutch School (possibly executed in Ireland), XVIII Century

226. A Rosewood Side Chair. A similar example in an American publication of 1902, still in print, is described as "undoubtedly an original Chippendale example."
Portuguese, XVIII Century

223. A Rococo Side Chair.
Lubeck, XVIII Century
Courtesy of the Museen der Hansestadt Lubeck

227. A Mahogany Side Chair. Once sold at a high figure as American.
Portuguese, XVIII Century

228. A Walnut Armchair.
North German, XVIII Century

FURNITURE RELATED TO THE FRENCH SCHOOL

224. A FRUITWOOD SETTEE. A related armchair in mahogany, and Dutch needlepoint, is exhibited at the Stadtisches Museum, The Hague. Dutch, XVIII Century

229. A MAHOGANY UPHOLSTERED ARMCHAIR. Dutch School, XVIII Century

230. A MAHOGANY UPHOLSTERED ARMCHAIR. Dutch, XVIII Century

A DIRECTORY OF ANTIQUE FURNITURE

231. A Mahogany Tea Comfort.
Dutch, XVIII Century

232. A Mahogany Torchere.
Dutch, XVIII Century

235. A Mahogany Tripod Table.
Dutch or Irish, XVIII Century

233. A Mahogany Tripod Table. By Lars Nordin, who also worked in the French taste, and for export.
Stockholm, XVIII Century
Courtesy of the Nordiska Museet, Stockholm

236. An Oak Bedside Table.
Dutch, XVIII Century

234. A Mahogany Tripod Table.
Danish or Pomeranian, XVIII Century

FURNITURE RELATED TO THE FRENCH SCHOOL

238. A Mahogany Drop-Leaf Table.
Dutch, XVIII Century

239. A Walnut Card Table. The frame reconditioned. West German or Dutch, XVIII Century

237. A Mahogany Tray-Top Table.
Dutch, XVIII Century

243. An Inland Kingwood Card Table. German, XVIII Century

A DIRECTORY OF ANTIQUE FURNITURE

241. A WALNUT CARD TABLE.
Dutch School, XVIII Century

240. A MAHOGANY CARD TABLE. The downward curve of leaf scrolls at the knees is a technique carried over in Irish work.

Dutch, XVIII Century

242. A MAHOGANY CARD TABLE.
Dutch or Irish, XVIII Century

FURNITURE RELATED TO THE FRENCH SCHOOL

244. A "George II" Gilded Center Table. Flemish or West German, XVIII Century

246. A "Chippendale" Pine Console Table. Schleswig Holstein, XVIII Century

245. A Gilded Center Table. Schleswig, XVIII Century
Courtesy of the Dansk Folkemuseum, Copenhagen

A DIRECTORY OF ANTIQUE FURNITURE

247. A Black Lacquer Bureau Dressing Table.
Ronnings Lackir-Industrie, Copenhagen, XVIII Century
Courtesy of the Dansk Folkemuseum, Copenhagen

248. A Black Lacquer Cabinet on Stand. Dutch, XVIII Century

249. A Coromandel Lacquer Cabinet. The stand supplied at this or another shipping point in Southern Asia. Chinese, Early XVIII Century

FURNITURE RELATED TO THE FRENCH SCHOOL

252. A WALNUT BLOCK-FRONT SECRETARY. Probably made in the region of Kiel. This favored New England front shaping was first employed in Germany and Denmark, not in Holland. Schleswig Holstein or North Germany, XVIII Century

250. A RED LACQUER SECRETARY. Dutch, XVIII Century

A DIRECTORY OF ANTIQUE FURNITURE

253. A BLACK LACQUER KNEEHOLE DESK. Chinese, XVIII Century

251. A WALNUT CHEST OF DRAWERS. With original brasses. North German, XVIII Century

254. A "GEORGE I PADOUK DESK." Dutch, XVIII Century

255. A WALNUT CHEST OF DRAWERS. Dutch, XVIII Century

257. A Walnut Secretary.
   German, XVIII Century

A DIRECTORY OF ANTIQUE FURNITURE

94

258. A "Queen Anne Red Walnut Secretary." Danish, XVIII Century

256. A Walnut Secretary. Compare the partition scrolls with Fig. 685. German, XVIII Century

FURNITURE RELATED TO THE ENGLISH SCHOOL

259. A GILDED WALL MIRROR.
Danish, XVIII Century

260. A GILDED WALL MIRROR.
Danish or Norwegian,
XVIII Century

A DIRECTORY OF ANTIQUE FURNITURE

261. A Walnut and Mahogany Side Chair. See Fig. 796.
Portuguese, XVIII Century

265. A Padouk Side Chair. With Chippendale splat, in the Gothic taste. Iberian, XVIII Century

262. A Mahogany Side Chair.
Hamburg, XVIII Century
Courtesy of the Museum für Kunst und Gewerbe, Hamburg

267. A Walnut Window Seat.
Viennese, XVIII Century

263. A Mahogany Armchair. With crest similar to English, Irish and Pennsylvania ladder-back examples.
North German, XVIII Century
Courtesy of the Museum für Kunst und Gewerbe, Hamburg

FURNITURE RELATED TO THE ENGLISH SCHOOL

268. A MAHOGANY ARMCHAIR. Of pre-Chippendale design.
Hamburg, XVIII Century
Courtesy of the Museum für Kunst und Gewerbe, Hamburg

271. A FRUITWOOD SIDE CHAIR.
Norwegian, XVIII Century
Courtesy of the Kunstindustrimuseet, Oslo

269. A MAHOGANY CORNER CHAIR. Scandinavian or North German,
XVIII Century
Courtesy of the Nordiska Museet, Stockholm

264. A MAHOGANY SIDE CHAIR. The Chippendale-pattern splat similar to designs in England, Ireland and Philadelphia.
North German, XVIII Century

266. A BEECH SIDE CHAIR. With monogram of Christian VII.
Altona, circa 1770
Courtesy of the Kunstindustrimuseet, Copenhagen

270. A MAHOGANY SIDE CHAIR. The Chippendale design of the splat similar to patterns used in England, Ireland and Philadelphia.
Hamburg, XVIII Century
Courtesy of the Museum für Kunst und Gewerbe, Hamburg

272. A Triple-Top Gaming Table.
Swedish, XVIII Century
Courtesy of the Nordiska Museet, Stockholm

273. An Olivewood and Kingwood "Harlequin" Table.
German, XVIII Century

275. A Mahogany Writing Table.
Swedish, XVIII Century
Courtesy of the Nordiska Museet, Stockholm

274. A Mahogany Card Table.
Swedish, XVIII Century
Courtesy of the Nordiska Museet, Stockholm

FURNITURE RELATED TO THE ENGLISH SCHOOL

277. A Mahogany Chest of Drawers. With oak carcase, and original mounts; the top drawer containing toilet compartments.
Copenhagen, XVIII Century
Courtesy of the Kunstindustrimuseet, Copenhagen

276. A Mahogany Chest of Drawers. The top drawer containing a writing slide and toilet compartments.
Schleswig Holstein, XVIII Century

278. A Mahogany Cupboard. The glass panels apparently added. See Fig. 822.
Dutch or Danish, XVIII Century

FURNITURE RELATED TO THE ENGLISH SCHOOL

279. A Gilded Wall Mirror.
Danish, XVIII Century

285. A Gilded Girandole. Italian carving, possibly executed in South Germany.
Italian School, XVIII Century

280. A Gilded Wall Mirror.
Danish, XVIII Century

283. A Gilded Wall Mirror.
Dutch, XVIII Century

284. A Gilded Wall Mirror.
Italian, XVIII Century

102 A DIRECTORY OF ANTIQUE FURNITURE

286. A Gilded Girandole.
German or Dutch, XVIII Century

282. A Parcel - Gilded Walnut Cabinet. Somewhat similar to Danish examples; oak lined. Illustrated here to show the typical mirror framing.
Hamburg, XVIII Century

281. A Gilded Pier Mirror.
Norwegian, XVIII Century

FURNITURE RELATED TO THE ENGLISH SCHOOL

103

287. A Parcel-Gilded Mahogany Pier Mirror.
Danish, XVIII Century

289. A Parcel-Gilded Walnut Pier Mirror.
North German, XVIII Century

288. A Parcel-Gilded Mahogany Pier Mirror.
Danish, XVIII Century

290. A Parcel-Gilded Walnut Pier Mirror. Danish, XVIII Century
Courtesy of the Schleswig-Holsteinisches Landesmuseum

291. A Parcel-Gilded Walnut Pier Mirror. A somewhat similar example is exhibited in the Metropolitan Museum of Art. Danish, XVIII Century

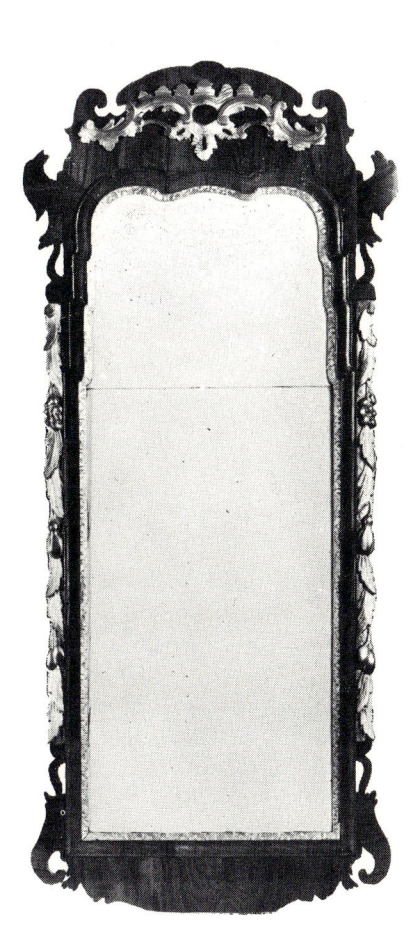

292. A Parcel-Gilded Walnut Pier Mirror. Danish or North German, XVIII Century

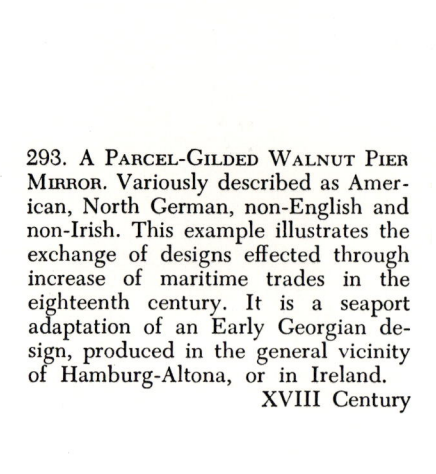

293. A Parcel-Gilded Walnut Pier Mirror. Variously described as American, North German, non-English and non-Irish. This example illustrates the exchange of designs effected through increase of maritime trades in the eighteenth century. It is a seaport adaptation of an Early Georgian design, produced in the general vicinity of Hamburg-Altona, or in Ireland.
XVIII Century

295. A "Marblehead Parcel-Gilded Walnut Washington Mirror." Restoration apparently includes the "Washington" head.
Danish, XVIII Century

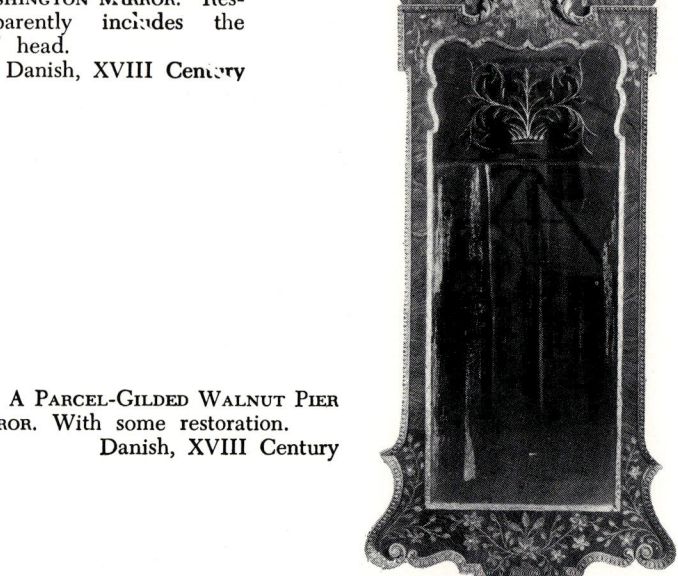

294. A Parcel-Gilded Walnut Pier Mirror. With some restoration.
Danish, XVIII Century

FURNITURE RELATED TO THE ENGLISH SCHOOL

296. A CUT AND ETCHED GLASS MIRROR. Swedish, XVIII Century
Courtesy of the Nordiska Museet, Stockholm

297. AN AMERICAN MAHOGANY KETTLE-BASE DRESSING MIRROR. With finely cut and etched looking glass imported from Sweden.
American and Swedish, XVIII Century
Courtesy of Ginsburg & Levy, Inc., New York City

299. AN EGLOMISÉ "COURTING MIRROR." With etched looking glass; painted border and crest plates.
Danish, XVIII Century

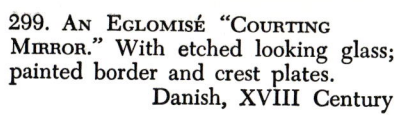

298. A PANEL-BORDER WALL MIRROR WITH EGLOMISÉ PAINTING. The crest plate finely painted in colors, gold and silver, depicting a courtier and blackamoor. A related example exhibited at the Metropolitan Museum of Art, as Chinese!
Danish, circa 1750

A DIRECTORY OF ANTIQUE FURNITURE

303. A Painted Settee. *En suite* with the preceding armchair.
German, XVIII Century

300. A Walnut Armchair.
German, XVIII Century

301. A Beech Armchair.
German, XVIII Century

304. A Painted and Gilded Armchair. Possibly made by an Italian craftsman in Berlin; the interlaced vine ornament carved on the front rail is similar to that on an Adam window seat at Chatsworth House.
German, XVIII Century

302. A Painted Armchair.
German, XVIII Century

305. A Painted and Gilded Armchair. A design sometimes described as Adam or Sheraton.
Italian, XVIII Century

FURNITURE RELATED TO THE ENGLISH SCHOOL

306. A Mahogany Side Chair. Of pre-Hepplewhite design.
Lubeck, XVIII Century
Courtesy of the Museen der Hansestadt Lubeck

307. An "Adam Mahogany Armchair." Apparently not in mahogany; the design related to English and Irish examples, and others produced in China and India.
Dutch School, XVIII Century

308. A Padouk Armchair.
Dutch School, XVIII Century

309. A "Heart-and-Shield" Side Chair. (See Fig. 580.)
German, XVIII Century
Courtesy of the Museum für Kunst und Gewerbe, Hamburg

A DIRECTORY OF ANTIQUE FURNITURE

310. A Mahogany Armchair. With splat shown in Hepplewhite's *Guide*. The example considered fraudulent by an English expert because of unrecognized disparities in its design.
North German, XVIII Century

311. A Mahogany Side Chair.
North German, circa 1800
Courtesy of the Museum für Kunst und Gewerbe, Hamburg

313. A Painted and Gilded Side Chair. Designs of this type were "not English enough" for traders in North Germany during the early years of this century. Berlin, circa 1787
Courtesy of the Schlossmuseum, Berlin

312. A Mahogany Side Chair.
North German, XVIII Century
Courtesy of the Museum für Kunst und Gewerbe, Hamburg

FURNITURE RELATED TO THE ENGLISH SCHOOL

314. A Mahogany Side Chair.
North German, XVIII Century

315. A Lyre-Back Side Chair.
North German, XVIII Century
Courtesy of the Museum für Kunst und Gewerbe, Hamburg

317. A Painted Side Chair.
Jacob Malmsten,
Stockholm, circa 1800
Courtesy of the Nordiska Museet, Stockholm

316. A Painted Side Chair.
Swedish, XVIII Century
Courtesy of the Nordiska Museet, Stockholm

318. A Painted and Decorated Side Chair. Described as probably Italian. Danish, circa 1800

A DIRECTORY OF ANTIQUE FURNITURE

319. A Mahogany Torchere.
Dutch, circa 1800

323. A Mahogany Trestle Stand with Drop Leaves. Similar designs were produced in Germany.
Swedish, Circa 1800
Courtesy of the Nordiska Museet, Stockholm

320. A Mahogany Torchere.
Dutch, Early XIX Century

322. A Mahogany Bedside Commode. Of Directoire-Sheraton design.
Swedish, Late XVIII Century
Courtesy of the Nordiska Museet, Stockholm

321. A Marquetry Portable Stand. Derived from Dutch examples.
Swedish, XVIII-XIX Century
Courtesy of the Nordiska Museet, Stockholm

324. A Curly Birch Occasional Table with Mahogany Finish.
German, circa 1800

FURNITURE RELATED TO THE ENGLISH SCHOOL

325. AN INLAID FRUITWOOD OCCASIONAL TABLE. The top centering Prince-of-Wales plumes.
Danish, Late XVIII Century
Courtesy of the Nationalmuseet, Copenhagen

326. A FRUITWOOD AND MAHOGANY CENTER TABLE. A type often accompanied by a decorative tray, to fit within the shallow gallery.
Danish or German, circa 1800

327. A MARQUETRY CENTER TABLE. From the Strogonoff Collection, Leningrad; described as English.
German, Late XVIII Century

328. A Mahogany Writing Table.
German, Late XVIII Century

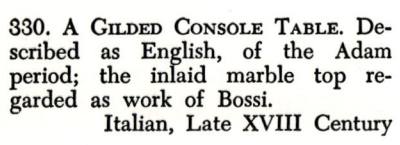

330. A Gilded Console Table. Described as English, of the Adam period; the inlaid marble top regarded as work of Bossi.
Italian, Late XVIII Century

329. A Mahogany Sideboard Table. With seal of the *Kongelige Meuble Magazin.* Copenhagen, circa 1790
Courtesy of the Kunstindustrimuseet, Copenhagen

FURNITURE RELATED TO THE ENGLISH SCHOOL

331. AN ADAM CITRONNIER MARQUETRY COMMODE. Inlaid in sycamore and tinted veneers; gilded metal traverse bands. Danish work throughout, related to both English and Irish designs. Copenhagen, Late XVIII Century
From the Royal Collection at Rosenborg Castle, Copenhagen

A DIRECTORY OF ANTIQUE FURNITURE

332. A Mahogany Chest of Drawers. German, XVIII Century

333. A Mahogany Chest of Drawers. Hamburg, circa 1800

334. A Mahogany Secretary.
Ｗest Indian, circa 1810

335. A Gilded Wall Mirror.
    Danish, XVIII Century

336. A Gilded Wall Mirror.
    German, XVIII Century

337. A Gilded and Painted Wall Mirror.   German, XVIII Century

338. A Gilded Wall Mirror.
    Dutch, XVIII Century

FURNITURE RELATED TO THE ENGLISH SCHOOL

339. A GILDED WALL MIRROR. Regarded as a Massachusetts example.
Dutch, XVIII Century

340. A LOUIS XVI GILDED PIER MIRROR. A French version of a popular Dutch theme. (Penn. Gazette, 5-12-1784, James Reynolds adv.: Just imported, a great variety of English, French and Dutch looking glasses.) See Fig. 474.
French, XVIII Century

341. A GILDED WALL MIRROR. With *eglomisé* panel.
Dutch, XVIII Century

343. A GILDED AND PAINTED WALL MIRROR. The emblems denoting Friendship with America. Such examples may have emanated from port towns in the Friesland areas.
Dutch School, Late XVIII Century

342. A GILDED WALL MIRROR. With *eglomisé* panels. With increases in shipping trades, and the rise of Freemasonry, northern Continental towns supplied their furniture with emblems of Fraternity, the figure of Hope with an anchor, mementos, etc.
Dutch School, Late XVIII Century

344. A Parcel-Gilded Fruitwood Wall Mirror. Schleswig Holstein, Late XVIII Century

345. A Parcel-Gilded Walnut Wall Mirror. Similar examples in the Metropolitan Museum of Art are exhibited as American.
Schleswig Holstein, Late XVIII Century

346. A Parcel-Gilded Walnut Wall Mirror.
Schleswig Holstein, circa 1800

347. A Parcel-Gilded Mahogany Wall Mirror. Described as American, circa 1785.
Danish, circa 1800

FURNITURE RELATED TO THE ENGLISH SCHOOL

348. A Carved Mahogany Side Chair. Variations of this, and the following design, were produced as far east as Danzig.
Hamburg, Late XVIII Century
Courtesy of the Museum für Kunst und Gewerbe, Hamburg

349. A Mahogany Side Chair.
Hamburg, Late XVIII Century
Courtesy of the Museum für Kunst und Gewerbe, Hamburg

350. A Mahogany Side Chair.
Hamburg, circa 1800
Courtesy of the Museum für Kunst und Gewerbe, Hamburg

351. A Mahogany Side Chair.
Hamburg, circa 1800
Courtesy of the Museum für Kunst und Gewerbe, Hamburg

352. A Mahogany Side Chair.
Hamburg, circa 1800
Courtesy of the Museum für Kunst und Gewerbe, Hamburg

353. A Mahogany Side Chair.
Hamburg, circa 1800
Courtesy of the Museum für Kunst und Gewerbe, Hamburg

354. A Mahogany Side Chair.
Hamburg, circa 1800
Courtesy of the Museum für Kunst und Gewerbe, Hamburg

355. A Mahogany Armchair.
Danish or North German, circa 1800

356. A Mahogany Side Chair.
Swedish, Late XVIII Century
Courtesy of the Nordiska Museet, Stockholm

358. A Painted and Decorated Beech Side Chair.
Danish, circa 1800
Courtesy of the Dansk Folkemuseum, Copenhagen

359. A Painted and Decorated Settee. Danish, circa 1810
Courtesy of the Kunstindustrimuseet, Oslo

FURNITURE RELATED TO THE ENGLISH SCHOOL

360. AN INLAID MAHOGANY ARMCHAIR. North German, circa 1815

361. A MAHOGANY SIDE CHAIR. Danish, circa 1815

357. A CANED-SEAT ARMCHAIR. The ebeneous wood between walnut and rosewood in appearance, when cut exposes heavy, jetlike veins with a consistency of crayon. Numbers of these models have appeared in America. Kenya Colony, East Africa; circa 1820

362. A PAINTED SIDE CHAIR. Swedish, circa 1815
Courtesy of the Nordiska Museet, Stockholm

363. A MAHOGANY FOLDING CHAIR. Convertible to library steps. Swedish, circa 1820
Courtesy of the Nordiska Museet, Stockholm

364. A Brass-Bound Fruitwood Wine Cooler. The same elliptical form also appearing in mahogany.
Dutch, circa 1800

365. A Work Table with Sewing Basket. Swedish, circa 1815
Courtesy of the Nordiska Museet, Stockholm

368. A Burl Maple and Ebonized Pedestal. German, circa 1820

366. A Mahogany Lyre Table. Probably Swedish, but similar to Danish designs, and to those of Norway at this time.
Scandinavian, circa 1820
Courtesy of the Dansk Folkemuseum, Copenhagen

367. A Rosewood Marquetry Console Pedestal.
German, circa 1810

FURNITURE RELATED TO THE ENGLISH SCHOOL

369. A Three-Tier Dumbwaiter.
Many finer stands of this type were made in Berlin and Vienna.
Swedish, circa 1820
Courtesy of the Nordiska Museet, Stockholm

370. A Mahogany Whatnot.
Swedish, circa 1840
Courtesy of the Nordiska Museet, Stockholm

371. A Mahogany Cheval Mirror.
With delicately cut and etched frieze panel. Swedish, circa 1815
Courtesy of the Nordiska Museet, Stockholm

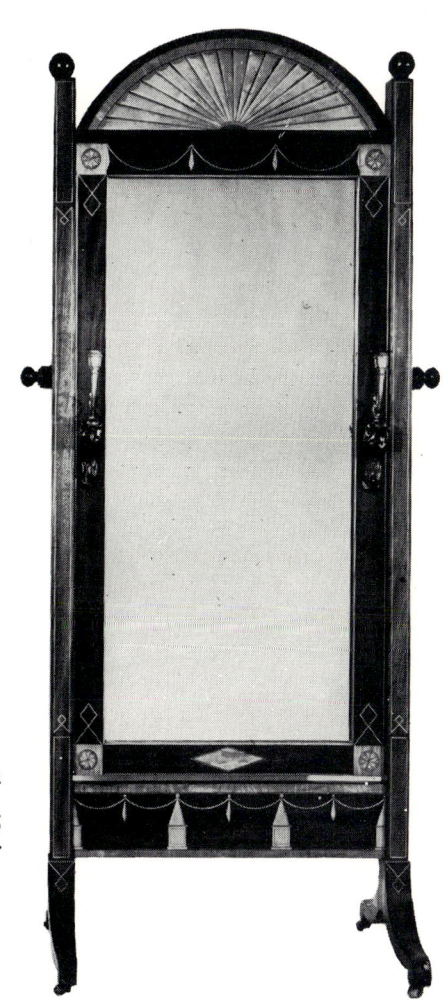

372. A Mahogany and Citronnier Cheval Mirror.
Danish, circa 1815
Courtesy of the Kunstindustrimuseet, Copenhagen

373. A Mahogany and Citronnier Sofa Table. Apparently made in Copenhagen or Flensburg.
From the Danish West Indies; circa 1820
Courtesy of Tyge Hvass, author of Mobler Fra Dansk Vestindien

374. A Rosewood Sofa Table. Danish, circa 1820

FURNITURE RELATED TO THE ENGLISH SCHOOL

378. A Mahogany Sideboard. With structural rails tenoned through the back. German, circa 1810

376. A Mahogany Dining Table.
Swedish, circa 1800
Courtesy of the Nordiska Museet, Stockholm

375. A Parcel-Gilded Mahogany Sofa Table. With typical lopers supporting the drop leaves.
Danish, circa 1830
Courtesy of the Dansk Folkemuseum, Copenhagen

380. A Mahogany Card Table.
Danish, circa 1820
Courtesy of Tyge Hvass, author of Mobler Fra Dansk Vestindien

377. A Rosewood Console Table.
Dutch, circa 1820

FURNITURE RELATED TO THE ENGLISH SCHOOL

379. A "SHERATON BONE-INLAID MAHOGANY SIDEBOARD." Formerly ascribed to Baltimore. Apparently of red *nara* wood.
Philippine Islands, circa 1820

381. A "REGENCY" GILDED CENTER TABLE. German, circa 1830

A DIRECTORY OF ANTIQUE FURNITURE

384. A Mahogany Chest of Drawers. With silver handles and escutcheons. Hamburg, circa 1810

382. A Rosewood Commode with Lacquer Decoration. Dutch, circa 1800

383. A "Sheraton" Mahogany Chest of Drawers. Hamburg, circa 1810

FURNITURE RELATED TO THE ENGLISH SCHOOL

386. An Inlaid Mahogany Secretary. The grilles of later date. North German, circa 1810

385. A Mahogany Chest of Drawers. The front swell formerly flanked by balusters, replaced by the existing terms in a poor attempt at conversion to a "rare" American example. West Indian, circa 1810

387. A "Regency" Mahogany Cabinet. With marble portrait medallions; the grilles apparently of later date. German, circa 1810-1820

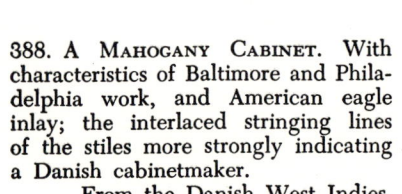

388. A Mahogany Cabinet. With characteristics of Baltimore and Philadelphia work, and American eagle inlay; the interlaced stringing lines of the stiles more strongly indicating a Danish cabinetmaker.
From the Danish West Indies, circa 1810
Courtesy of Tyge Hvass, author of Mobler Fra Dansk Vestindien

FURNITURE RELATED TO THE ENGLISH SCHOOL

389. A Gilded Wall Mirror.
Bremen, circa 1810

390. A Gilded Pier Mirror.
North German, circa 1820

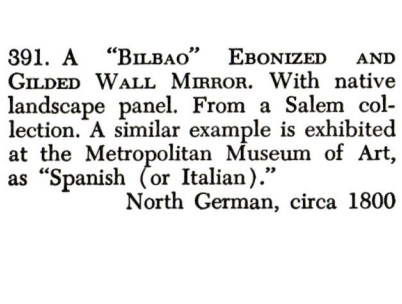

392. A "Bilbao Parcel - Gilded Kingwood Wall Mirror." With native landscape painting.
North German, circa 1800

394. A "Bilbao" Wall Mirror. A suburban rendition; the frame as well as the colonottes in rose-tinted alabaster. Painted tole panel.
North German, circa 1810

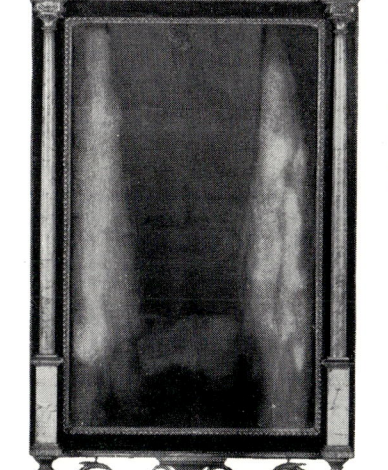

391. A "Bilbao" Ebonized and Gilded Wall Mirror. With native landscape panel. From a Salem collection. A similar example is exhibited at the Metropolitan Museum of Art, as "Spanish (or Italian)."
North German, circa 1800

393. A "Bilbao" Parcel - Gilded Wall Mirror. With native landscape painting.
North German, circa 1800

FURNITURE RELATED TO THE ENGLISH SCHOOL

397. A GILDED WALL MIRROR.
Swedish, circa 1820
Courtesy of the Nordiska Museet, Stockholm

398. A BRONZE AND GILDED BRONZE WALL CLOCK.
Stockholm, circa 1800
Courtesy of the Nordiska Museet, Stockholm

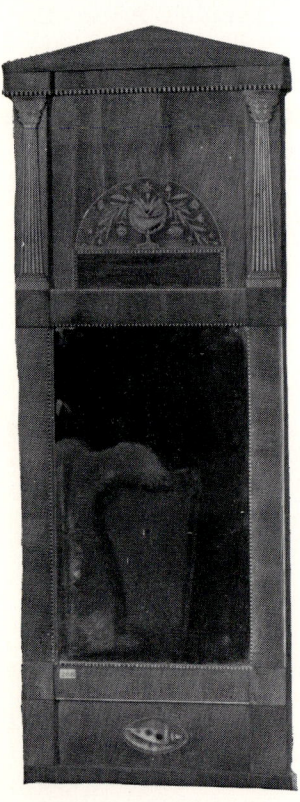

395. A FRUITWOOD PIER MIRROR.
Danish or North German, circa, 1820

396. A MAHOGANY PIER MIRROR.
Swedish, circa 1820
Courtesy of the Nordiska Museet, Stockholm

FRENCH FURNITURE,
BASED ON PARIS DESIGNS

FRENCH FURNITURE

399. A LOUIS XIV GILDED ARMCHAIR. French, circa 1700

400. A LOUIS XIV GILDED TORCHERE. French, circa 1700

401. A LOUIS XIV GILDED CONSOLE TABLE. French, circa 1700
Mary S. Harkness Collection. Photograph by Taylor & Dull

402. A LOUIS XIV GILDED PIER MIRROR. French, circa 1700

A DIRECTORY OF ANTIQUE FURNITURE

403. A Régence Walnut Fauteuil.
French, Early XVIII Century

404. A Régence Beech Bergère.
French, Early XVIII Century

405. A Louis XV Walnut Fauteuil.
French, XVIII Century

406. A Louis XV Beech Fauteuil.
French, XVIII Century

409. A Louis XV Beech Fauteuil.
French, XVIII Century

408. A Louis XV Painted Fauteuil.
French, XVIII Century

FRENCH FURNITURE

135

407. A Louis XV Beech Canapé.
French, XVIII Century

412. A Louis XV-XVI Beech Fauteuil. French, XVIII Century

411. A Louis XV Painted Bergère.
French, XVIII Century

410. A Louis XV Walnut Bergère.
French, XVIII Century

413. A Louis XV-XVI Gilded Lit à La Turque.
French, XVIII Century

136 A DIRECTORY OF ANTIQUE FURNITURE

414. A Louis XV Tulipwood
Marquetry Occasional Table.
French, XVIII Century

415. A Louis XV Tulipwood
Marquetry Petit Table à Écrire.
French, XVIII Century

418. A Louis XV Acajou
Marquetry Occasional Table.
French, XVIII Century

416. A Louis XV Kingwood
Marquetry Table de Dame.
French, XVIII Century

417. A Louis XV Amaranth
Marquetry Table de Dame.
French, XVIII Century

FRENCH FURNITURE

419. A LOUIS XV TULIPWOOD
MARQUETRY TABLE À ROGNON.
French, XVIII Century
Mrs. Orme Wilson Collection.
Photograph by Taylor & Dull

420. A LOUIS XV-XVI TULIPWOOD
PARQUETRY TABLE DE DAME.
French, XVIII Century

421. A LOUIS XV-XVI TULIPWOOD
MARQUETRY TABLE À ROGNON.
French, XVIII Century

422. A LOUIS XV KINGWOOD
MARQUETRY BUREAU DE DAME.
French, XVIII Century

138 A DIRECTORY OF ANTIQUE FURNITURE

423. A Louis XV-XVI Marquetry Bureau à Cylindre.
French, XVIII Century

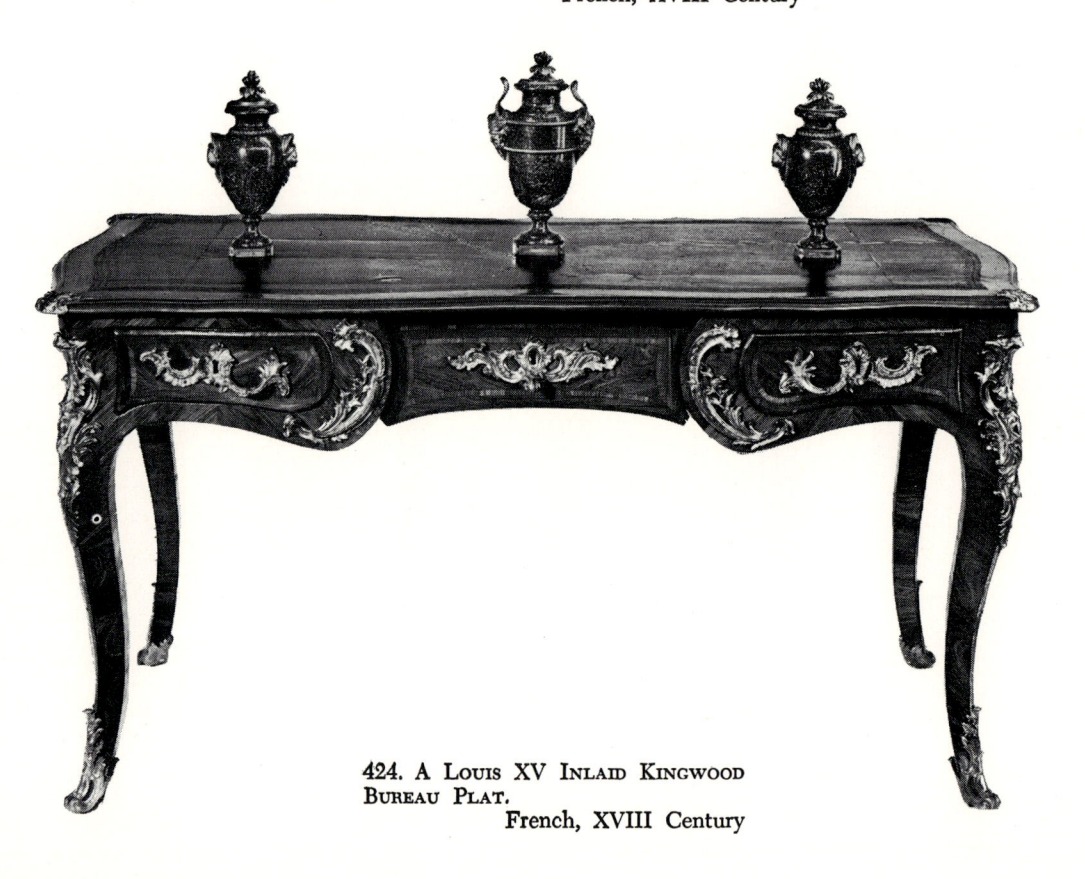

424. A Louis XV Inlaid Kingwood Bureau Plat.
French, XVIII Century

FRENCH FURNITURE

425. A Louis XV Carved Oak Console Table.
French, XVIII Century

426. A Louis XV-XVI Gilded Console Table.
French, XVIII Century

427. A Louis XV Amaranth
Marquetry Commode.
French, XVIII Century

428. A Louis XV Black and Gold
Lacquer Commode.
French, XVIII Century

429. A Louis XV Tulipwood
Parquetry Commode. Style of Cressent.
French, XVIII Century

FRENCH FURNITURE

430. A Louis XV Tulipwood Marquetry Commode.
　　　French, XVIII Century

431. A Louis XV Amaranth Marquetry Commode.
　　　French, XVIII Century

432. A Louis XV Inlaid Kingwood Commode.
　　　French, XVIII Century

435. A Louis XV Bronze Doré Cartel. French, XVIII Century

434. A Louis XV Bronze Doré Cartel. French, XVIII Century

433. A Louis XV Inlaid Tulipwood Cabinet.
French, XVIII Century

FRENCH FURNITURE

436. A Louis XV-XVI Gilded Bergère.   French, XVIII Century

438. A Louis XVI Painted Canapé.
French, XVIII Century

437. A Louis XVI Painted Fauteuil.   French, XVIII Century

440. A Louis XVI Beech Chaffeuse.   French, XVIII Century
Dr. Leo Kessel Collection.
Photograph by Taylor & Dull

439. A Louis XVI Painted Fauteuil.   French, XVIII Century
Mrs. Orme Wilson Collection.
Photograph by Taylor & Dull

441. A Louis XVI Gilded Voyeuse.
French, XVIII Century

A DIRECTORY OF ANTIQUE FURNITURE

442. A LOUIS XVI WALNUT
FAUTEUIL. French, XVIII Century
*Mrs. Orme Wilson Collection.
Photograph by Taylor & Dull*

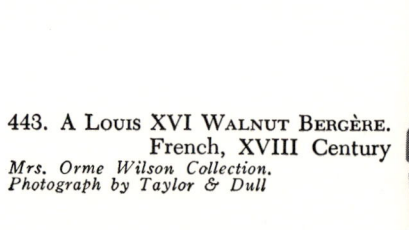

443. A LOUIS XVI WALNUT BERGÈRE.
French, XVIII Century
*Mrs. Orme Wilson Collection.
Photograph by Taylor & Dull*

446. A LOUIS XVI PAINTED CANAPÉ.
French, XVIII Century

444. A LOUIS XVI PAINTED BERGÈRE.
French, XVIII Century

445. A LOUIS XVI PAINTED
FAUTEUIL. French, XVIII Century

FRENCH FURNITURE

145

447. A LOUIS XVI PAINTED
FAUTEUIL. Style of Georges Jacob.
French, XVIII Century

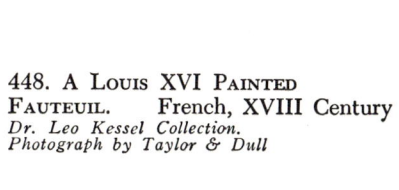

448. A LOUIS XVI PAINTED
FAUTEUIL.   French, XVIII Century
Dr. Leo Kessel Collection.
Photograph by Taylor & Dull

449. A LOUIS XVI PAINTED CANAPÉ.
French, XVIII Century
Princess Charles Murat Collection.
Photograph by Taylor & Dull

451. A LOUIS XVI DIRECTOIRE
PAINTED MARQUISE.
French, XVIII Century

450. A LOUIS XVI DIRECTOIRE
PAINTED BERGÈRE.
French, XVIII Century

146 A DIRECTORY OF ANTIQUE FURNITURE

452. A Louis XV-XVI Tulipwood Petit Commode.
French, XVIII Century

453. A Louis XVI Tulipwood Marquetry Petit Table-Gueridon.
French, XVIII Century

454. A Louis XVI Marquetry Chiffonnière.
French, XVIII Century

455. A Louis XVI Acajou Marquetry Chiffonnière.
French, XVIII Century
Mary S. Harkness Collection.
Photograph by Taylor & Dull

FRENCH FURNITURE

456. A LOUIS XVI TULIPWOOD
MARQUETRY TABLE À MILIEU.
French, XVIII Century
*Mary S. Harkness Collection.
Photograph by Taylor & Dull*

457. A LOUIS XVI KINGWOOD TABLE
À MILIEU.   French, XVIII Century

458. A LOUIS XVI CITRONNIER TABLE
À ÉCRIRE.   French, XVIII Century
*Mrs. Orme Wilson Collection.
Photograph by Taylor & Dull*

459. A Louis XVI Tulipwood Marquetry Bonheur-du-Jour. Style of Charles Topino.
French, XVIII Century

461. A Louis XVI Tulipwood Parquetry Bonheur-du-Jour.
French, XVIII Century

460. A Louis XVI Citronnier Parquetry Bureau à Cylindre.
French, XVIII Century

FRENCH FURNITURE

149

462. A LOUIS XVI EBONY BUREAU PLAT. Style of Philippe Claude Montigny. French, XVIII Century

463. A LOUIS XVI GILDED CONSOLE-ENCOIGNURE. French, XVIII Century

464. A LOUIS XVI DIRECTOIRE GILDED CONSOLE TABLE. French, XVIII Century

150 A DIRECTORY OF ANTIQUE FURNITURE

465. A Louis XVI Acajou and Ebony Desserte. French, XVIII Century

466. A Louis XVI Acajou and Ebony Commode-Desserte. French, XVIII Century

FRENCH FURNITURE

151

468. A Louis XVI Tulipwood and Amaranth Commode.
French, XVIII Century

467. A Louis XVI Amaranth and Sycamore Marquetry Commode.
Style of Jean-Francois Leleu.
French, XVIII Century

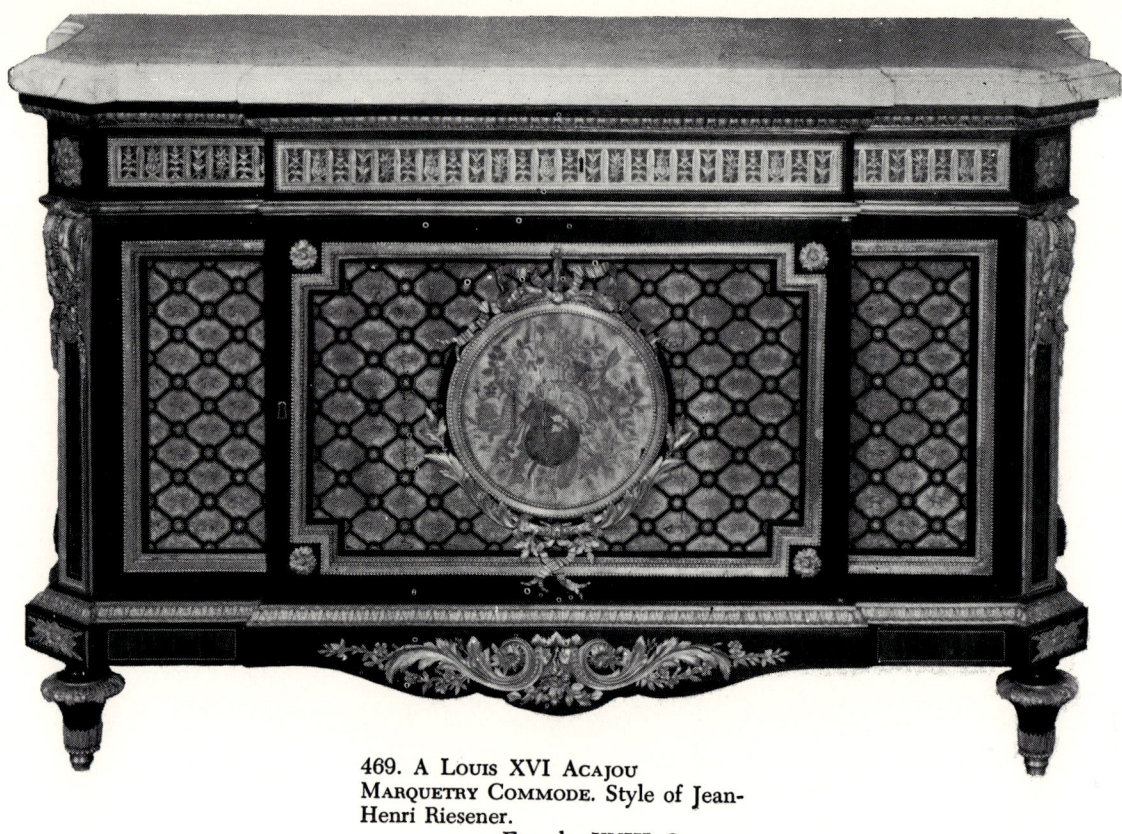

469. A Louis XVI Acajou Marquetry Commode. Style of Jean-Henri Riesener.
French, XVIII Century

470. A Louis XVI Acajou Commode.
Style of Jean-Henri Riesener.
French, XVIII Century
Mrs. Orme Wilson Collection.
Photograph by Taylor & Dull

FRENCH FURNITURE

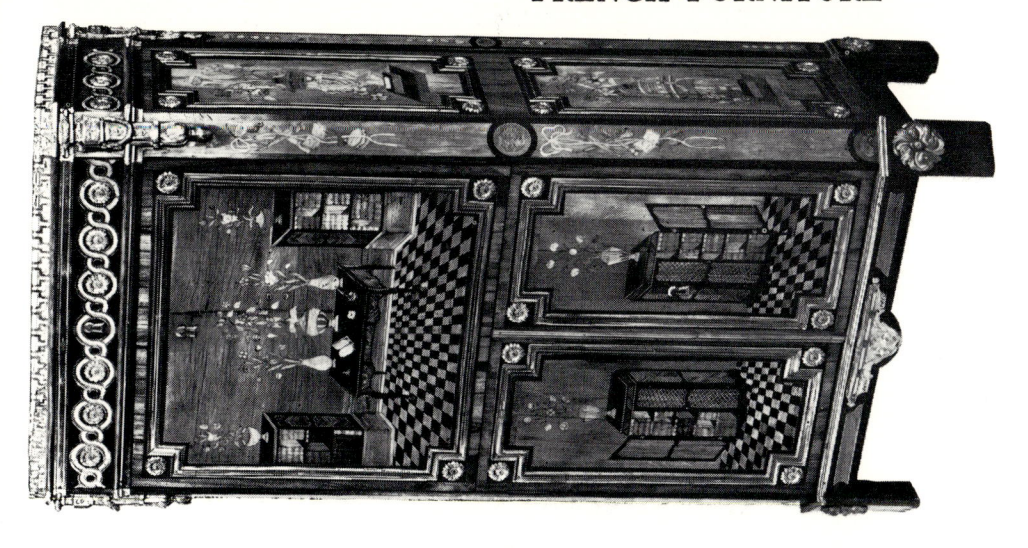

473. A LOUIS XVI MARQUETRY SECRÉTAIRE À ABATTANT. Style of Pierre Roussel.
French, XVIII Century
Mrs. Orme Wilson Collection.
Photograph by Taylor & Dull

472. A LOUIS XVI MARQUETRY SECRÉTAIRE À ABATTANT.
French, XVIII Century

471. A LOUIS XVI MARQUETRY SECRÉTAIRE À ABATTANT.
French, XVIII Century

A DIRECTORY OF ANTIQUE FURNITURE

474. A Louis XVI Gilded Pier Mirror.   French, XVIII Century

475. A Louis XVI Bronze Doré Cartel and Baromètre.
French, XVIII Century

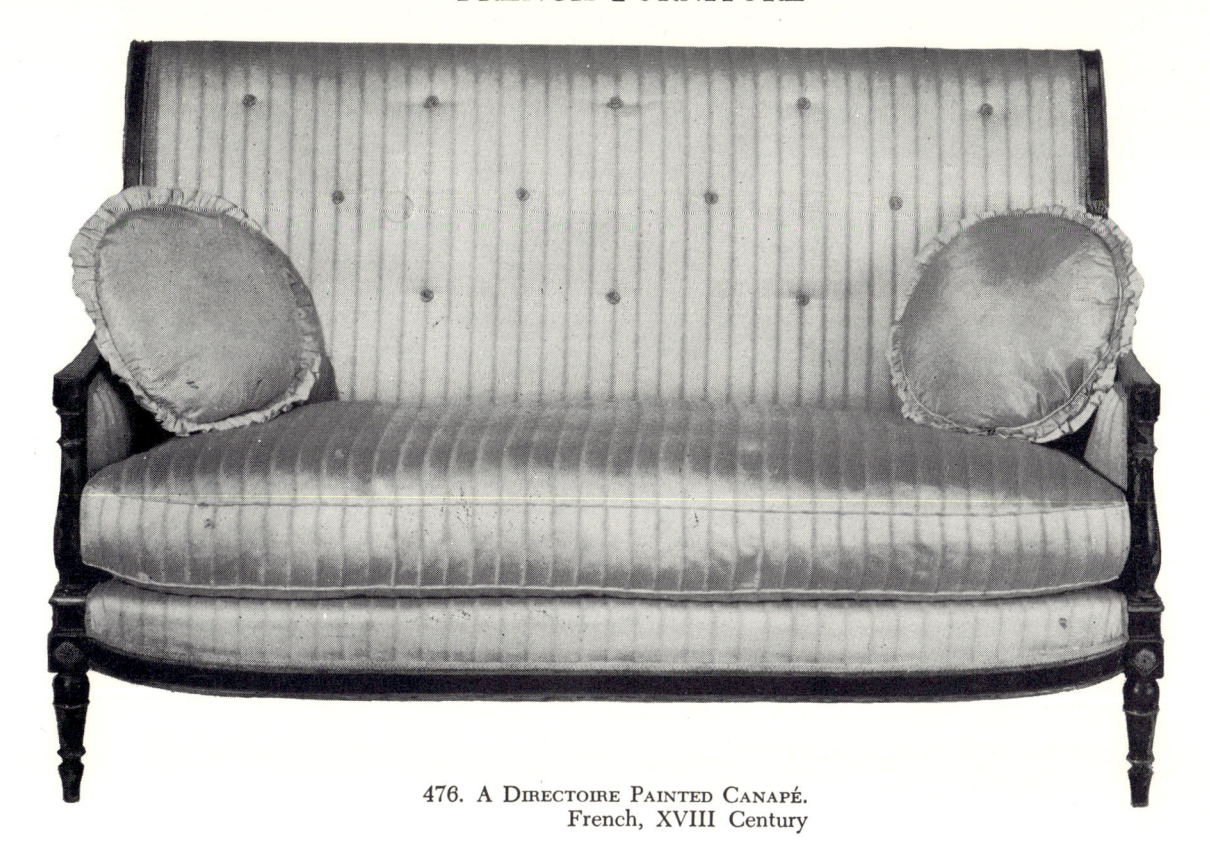

FRENCH FURNITURE

476. A Directoire Painted Canapé.
French, XVIII Century

477. A Directoire Acajou
Fauteuil. French, XVIII Century

478. A Consulate-Empire Acajou
Fauteuil.
French, XVIII-XIX Century

156 — A DIRECTORY OF ANTIQUE FURNITURE

479. A Directoire Thuyawood, Bronze Doré and Sèvres Porcelain Gueridon.
French, Late XVIII Century

480. A Directoire Bronze Doré and Marble Gueridon.
French, XVIII-XIX Century

481. A Directoire Acajou Bouillotte Table.
French, Late XVIII Century

482. A Directoire Acajou "Serviteur Fidèle."
French, Late XVIII Century

FRENCH FURNITURE

483. A DIRECTOIRE ACAJOU
COMMODE-DESSERTE.
French, Late XVIII Century

484. A DIRECTOIRE ACAJOU
DESSERTE.
French, Late XVIII Century

158 A DIRECTORY OF ANTIQUE FURNITURE

485. A Directoire Acajou Commode.
French, Late XVIII Century

487. A Directoire Painted Wall Mirror.
French, Late XVIII Century

486. A Directoire Acajou Secrétaire à Abattant.
French, Late XVIII Century

FRENCH FURNITURE 159

488. An Empire Acajou Fauteuil.
French, circa 1810

489. An Empire Acajou Fauteuil.
French, circa 1810

490. An Empire Acajou Table à
Ouvrage.   French, circa 1810

491. An Empire Acajou Table-
Gueridon.   French, circa 1810

493. An Empire Acajou Secrétaire a Abattant. French, circa 1810

492. An Empire Acajou Commode. French, circa 1810

FRENCH FURNITURE

495. A Restauration "Watered" Ash Lit en Bateau. French, circa 1830

496. A Restauration Burl Ash Commode. French, circa 1830

494. A Restauration Parcel-Gilded Acajou Fauteuil. French, circa 1830

ENGLISH FURNITURE,
BASED ON LONDON DESIGNS

ENGLISH FURNITURE

497. A "William III" Walnut Side Chair. Probably made by a Dutch chair-maker employed in London.
English, Early XVIII Century

498. An Inlaid Walnut Desk with Gate-Leg Frame.
English, circa 1700

499. A Walnut Oysterwood and Marquetry Side Table.
English, Late XVII Century

501. A Walnut Marquetry Cabinet. English, Late XVII Century
Mary S. Harkness Collection
Photograph by Taylor & Dull

500. A Walnut Oysterwood and Marquetry Fall-Front Writing Cabinet. English, Late XVII Century

502. A Queen Anne Walnut Side Chair.
English, Early XVIII Century
Mrs. Solomon R. Guggenheim Collection.
Photograph by Taylor & Dull

503. A Queen Anne Walnut Side Chair.
English, Early XVIII Century

504. A Queen Anne Walnut Side Chair.
English, Early XVIII Century
Mrs. Solomon R. Guggenheim Collection.
Photograph by Taylor & Dull

505. A Queen Anne Walnut Side Chair.
English, Early XVIII Century

ENGLISH FURNITURE

506. A Walnut Guild Armchair.
English, Early XVIII Century
Mrs. Middleton S. Burrill Collection.
Photograph by Taylor & Dull

507. A Queen Anne Walnut Wing Chair.
English, Early XVIII Century

508. A Queen Anne Walnut Settee.
English, Early XVIII Century

A DIRECTORY OF ANTIQUE FURNITURE

509. A Walnut Card Table.
English, Early XVIII Century

510. An Inlaid Walnut Side Table.
English, Early XVIII Century

511. A Queen Anne Walnut Side Table.
English, Early XVIII Century
Florence H. Crane Collection   *Photograph by Taylor & Dull*

ENGLISH FURNITURE

512. A Queen Anne Walnut and Oyster Parquetry Fall–Front Writing Cabinet.
English, Early XVIII Century

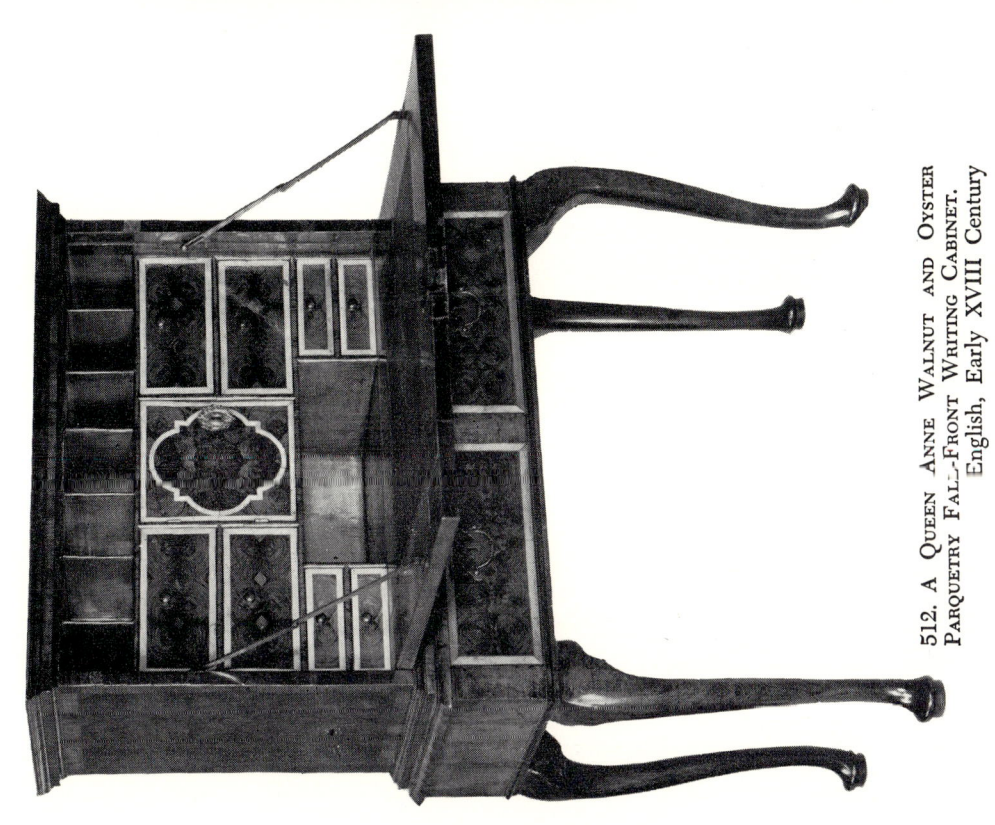

513. A Queen Anne Walnut Secretary.
English, Early XVIII Century
Victoria & Albert Museum, Crown Copyright

A DIRECTORY OF ANTIQUE FURNITURE

516. A Queen Anne Gilded Gesso Pier Mirror.
English, Early XVIII Century

515. An Inlaid Walnut Cabinet.
English, Early XVIII Century
*Robert J. Dunham Collection.
Photograph by Taylor & Dull*

514. A Queen Anne Walnut Secretary.
English, Early XVIII Century

ENGLISH FURNITURE

517. AN EARLY GEORGIAN MAHOGANY STOOL.
English, XVIII Century

518. AN EARLY GEORGIAN WALNUT SIDE CHAIR.
English, XVIII Century

519. AN EARLY GEORGIAN WALNUT ARMCHAIR. The lion heads resembling finials and arm terminals of Dutch chairs made during the Baroque period in that country.
English, XVIII Century

520. AN EARLY GEORGIAN MAHOGANY AND NEEDLEPOINT SIDE CHAIR.
English, XVIII Century

521. AN EARLY GEORGIAN MAHOGANY STRADDLE CHAIR.   English, XVIII Century

522. AN EARLY GEORGIAN WALNUT UPHOLSTERED OPEN-ARM EASY CHAIR. English, Early XVIII Century
*Florence H. Crane Collection.
Photograph by Taylor & Dull*

523. AN EARLY GEORGIAN MAHOGANY WING CHAIR. English, XVIII Century
*Carl von Seidlitz Collection.
Photograph by Taylor & Dull*

524. AN EARLY GEORGIAN WALNUT WING CHAIR. English, XVIII Century
*Dr. Leo Kessel Collection.
Photograph by Taylor & Dull*

525. AN EARLY GEORGIAN WALNUT AND NEEDLEPOINT SETTEE. English, XVIII Century

ENGLISH FURNITURE

526. A Mahogany Tripod Table.
English, XVIII Century

528. A Mahogany and Needlepoint Pole Screen. Apparently of Yorkshire origin.
British Isles, XVIII Century
J. P. Argenti Collection.
Photograph by Taylor & Dull

527. A Mahogany Tripod Table.
British Isles, XVIII Century

529. An Early Georgian Walnut Pedestal Desk.
English, XVIII Century
Florence H. Crane Collection. Photograph by Taylor & Dull

172 A DIRECTORY OF ANTIQUE FURNITURE

531. AN EARLY GEORGIAN WALNUT CARD TABLE.
English, XVIII Century

533. A GEORGE II GILDED AND PAINTED EAGLE CONSOLE.
English, XVIII Century

532. AN EARLY GEORGIAN MAHOGANY SIDE TABLE.
English, XVIII Century
Carl von Seidlitz Collection.
Photograph by Taylor & Dull

ENGLISH FURNITURE

534. A Walnut Chest of Drawers.
British, XVIII Century

530. An Early Georgian Walnut Side Table.
British, XVIII Century
Dr. Leo Kessel Collection.
Photograph by Taylor & Dull

535. A Mahogany Kneehole Writing Table.
English, XVIII Century

536. A George II Carved and Gilded Wood and Gesso Pier Mirror. English, XVIII Century

537. A George II Parcel-Gilded Walnut Pier Mirror. English, XVIII Century

538. A George II Parcel-Gilded Walnut Wall Mirror. English, XVIII Century
Victoria & Albert Museum. Crown Copyright.

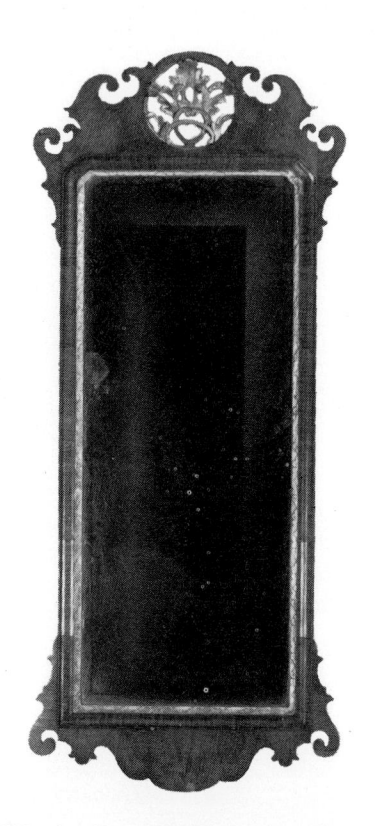

539. A George II Parcel-Gilded Walnut Wall Mirror. English, XVIII Century

ENGLISH FURNITURE

540. A Mahogany Upholstered Armchair.
British Isles, XVIII Century

541. A Mahogany Window Seat.
English, XVIII Century

542. A Mahogany Upholstered Settee.
English, XVIII Century

A DIRECTORY OF ANTIQUE FURNITURE

543. A Chippendale Mahogany Side Chair. Related to Philadelphia and Irish designs; excellence in carving of this type invariably prompts decisions against Irish work.
British Isles, XVIII Century

544. A Chippendale Mahogany Side Chair.
British Isles, XVIII Century

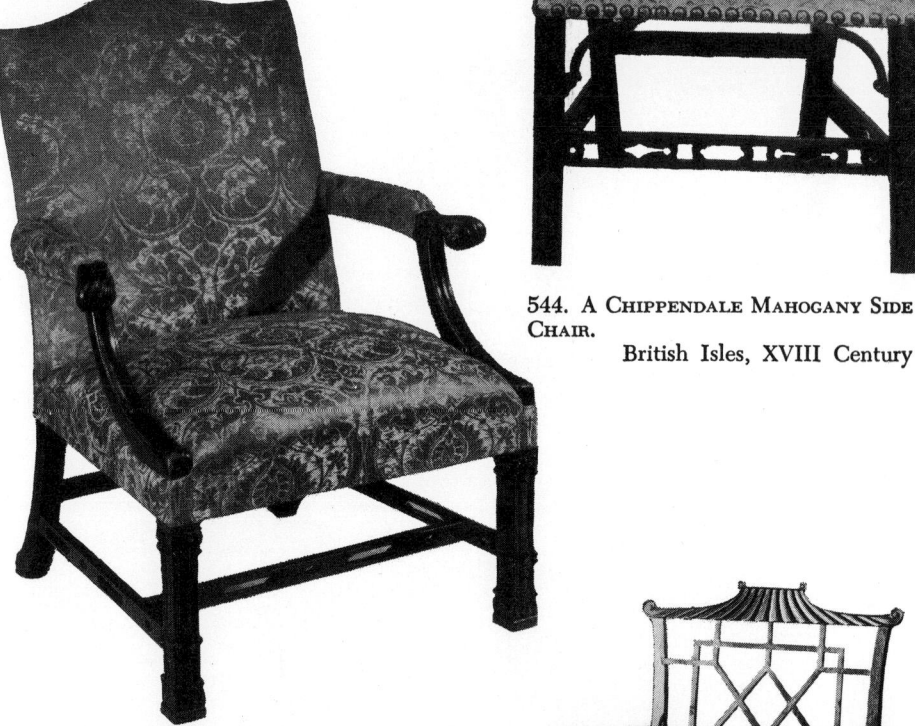

547. A Chippendale Mahogany Upholstered Armchair. Related to Philadelphia, and Irish designs.
British Isles, XVIII Century

545. A Mahogany Lattice-Back Side Chair.
English, XVIII Century

546. A Mahogany Armchair.
English, XVIII Century
Courtesy of Arthur S. Vernay, Inc., New York City

ENGLISH FURNITURE

548. A Chippendale Mahogany Wing Chair.
English, XVIII Century

549. A Chippendale Mahogany Wing Chair.
English, XVIII Century

550. A Chippendale Mahogany Settee.
English, XVIII Century

551. A Chippendale Mahogany Urn Stand.
English, XVIII Century

552. A Chippendale Mahogany Tripod Table.
English, XVIII Century
Robert J. Dunham Collection.
Photograph by Taylor & Dull

554. A Chippendale Mahogany Tripod Table.
English, XVIII Century
Mary S. Harkness Collection.
Photograph by Taylor & Dull

553. A Chippendale Mahogany Tripod Table.
English, XVIII Century

556. A Chippendale Mahogany and Mortlake Tapestry Pole Screen. English, XVIII Century

555. A Chippendale Mahogany Torchere. English, XVIII Century

ENGLISH FURNITURE

557. A CHIPPENDALE MAHOGANY SILVER TABLE. English, XVIII Century
Robert J. Dunham Collection.
Photograph by Taylor & Dull

558. A CHIPPENDALE MAHOGANY DROP-LEAF TABLE. British Isles, XVIII Century
Carl von Seidlitz Collection.
Photograph by Taylor & Dull

559. A MAHOGANY WRITING TABLE. British Isles, Late XVIII Century

560. A CHIPPENDALE GILDED CONSOLE. English, XVIII Century
Courtesy of Arthur S. Vernay, Inc., New York City

180 A DIRECTORY OF ANTIQUE FURNITURE

563. A Chippendale Mahogany Chest of Drawers. English, XVIII Century

561. A Chippendale Mahogany Commode. British Isles, XVIII Century
J. P. Argenti Collection   Photograph by Taylor & Dull

ENGLISH FURNITURE

564. A Chippendale Mahogany Secretary. English, XVIII Century

562. A Chippendale Kingwood Marquetry Cabinet. Indicating the work of foreign craftsmen in England; the marquetry and appliqués are related to work in Paris, Eastern France, and Germany. English, XVIII Century

565. A Chippendale Mahogany Bookcase.
English, XVIII Century

566. A Chippendale Mahogany Bookcase.
English, XVIII Century

184   A DIRECTORY OF ANTIQUE FURNITURE

567. A CHIPPENDALE GILDED WALL MIRROR.
English, XVIII Century
Courtesy of Needham's Antiques, Inc., New York City

569. A CHIPPENDALE GILDED GIRANDOLE.
English, XVIII Century
Carl von Seidlitz Collection.
Photograph by Taylor & Dull

570. A CHIPPENDALE GILDED MIRROR APPLIQUÉ.   English, XVIII Century

568. A CHIPPENDALE GILDED WALL MIRROR.
Style of Thomas Johnson.
English, XVIII Century
Carl von Seidlitz Collection.
Photograph by Taylor & Dull

ENGLISH FURNITURE

185

572. A Hepplewhite Mahogany Upholstered Armchair.
English, XVIII Century
Courtesy of Needham's Antiques, Inc., New York City

571. A Hepplewhite Mahogany Stool. Accepted terminology associates Hepplewhite's name with these "French" designs, though he showed little feeling for such cabriole forms . . . generally antedating his publications. English, XVIII Century

573. A Hepplewhite Mahogany "Cabriolet" Armchair.
English, XVIII Century

574. An Adam Gilded Settee. English, XVIII Century

576. A Hepplewhite Mahogany Armchair. English, XVIII Century

575. An Adam Beech Armchair. Typifying work executed by foreign craftsmen in England and Ireland. English, XVIII Century
Robert J. Dunham Collection.
Photograph by Taylor & Dull

577. A Hepplewhite Mahogany Armchair. English, XVIII Century
J. P. Argenti Collection.
Photograph by Taylor & Dull

579. A Hepplewhite Painted Armchair. English, XVIII Century
Courtesy of Arthur S. Vernay, Inc., New York City

580. A Hepplewhite Mahogany Armchair. English, XVIII Century

578. A Hepplewhite Mahogany Armchair. English, XVIII Century

ENGLISH FURNITURE

581. A Hepplewhite Mahogany Armchair. English, XVIII Century

582. A Hepplewhite Mahogany Side Chair. English, XVIII Century

585. A Hepplewhite Mahogany Bergère. Hepplewhite's form of "Barjier chair." English, XVIII Century

583. A Hepplewhite Mahogany English, XVIII Century

584. A Hepplewhite Mahogany Armchair. A favored model in Great Britain and North Germany. English, XVIII Century

588. A Mahogany Wing Chair.
English, XVIII Century
Florence H. Crane Collection.
Photograph by Taylor & Dull

587. A Hepplewhite Mahogany Wing Chair.
English, XVIII Century

586. A Hepplewhite Mahogany Bergère. English, XVIII Century

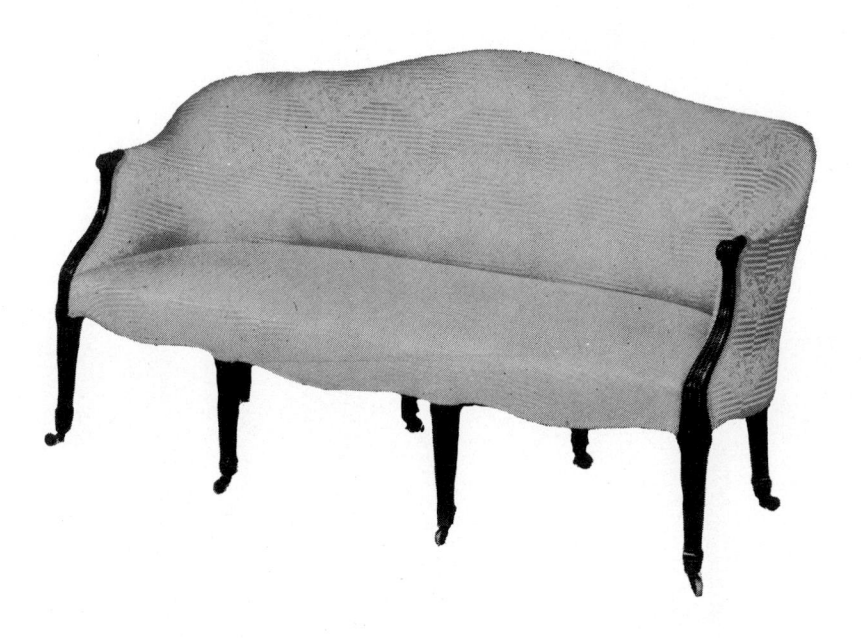

589. A Hepplewhite Mahogany Settee.
English, XVIII Century

ENGLISH FURNITURE

590. A Hepplewhite Mahogany Urn Stand.
English, XVIII Century

593. A Hepplewhite Mahogany Pembroke Table.
English, XVIII Century

592. A Hepplewhite Mahogany Pembroke Table.
English, XVIII Century

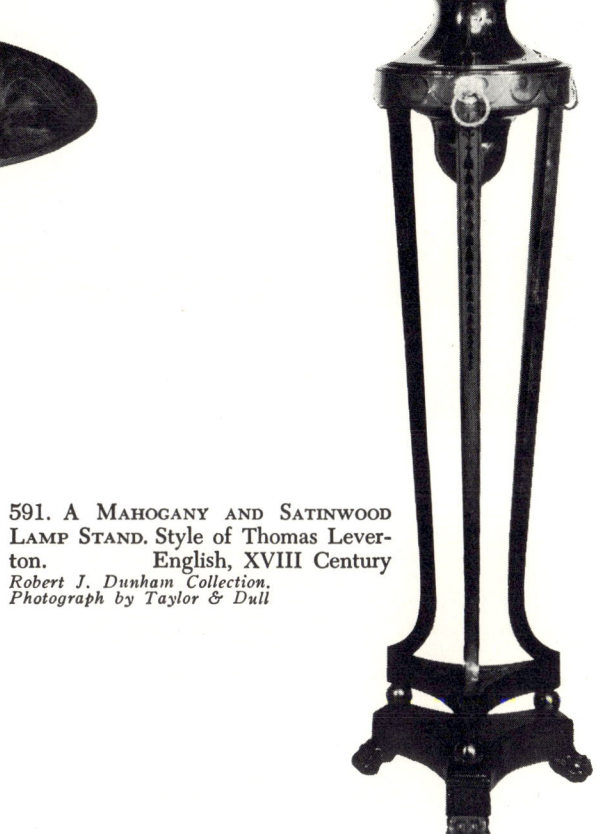

591. A Mahogany and Satinwood Lamp Stand. Style of Thomas Leverton.
English, XVIII Century
Robert J. Dunham Collection.
Photograph by Taylor & Dull

594. A Mahogany Pedestal Writing Desk.
English, XVIII Century
Courtesy of Needham's Antiques, Inc., New York City

595. A Mahogany Serpentine Pedestal Writing Desk.
Style of Thomas Shearer.   English, XVIII Century
Courtesy of Needham's Antiques, Inc., New York City

ENGLISH FURNITURE

596. A HEPPLEWHITE MAHOGANY CARD TABLE.
English, XVIII Century

597. A HEPPLEWHITE GILDED SIDE TABLE.
With inlaid and decorated satinwood top.
English, XVIII Century
Robert J. Dunham Collection.
Photograph by Taylor & Dull

598. AN ADAM MAHOGANY SIDE TABLE.
English, XVIII Century
J. P. Argenti Collection.
Photograph by Taylor & Dull

599. A Mahogany Sideboard   English, XVIII Century

600. A Mahogany Sideboard.   English, XVIII Century

ENGLISH FURNITURE

602. A Hepplewhite Mahogany Chest of Drawers.
English, XVIII Century

601. A Hepplewhite Olivewood and Palisander Marquetry Commode. German examples also feature the fitting of an interior nest of drawers. From Castle Moyle, County Kerry, Ireland. British Isles, XVIII Century

Robert J. Dunham Collection.
Photograph by Taylor & Dull

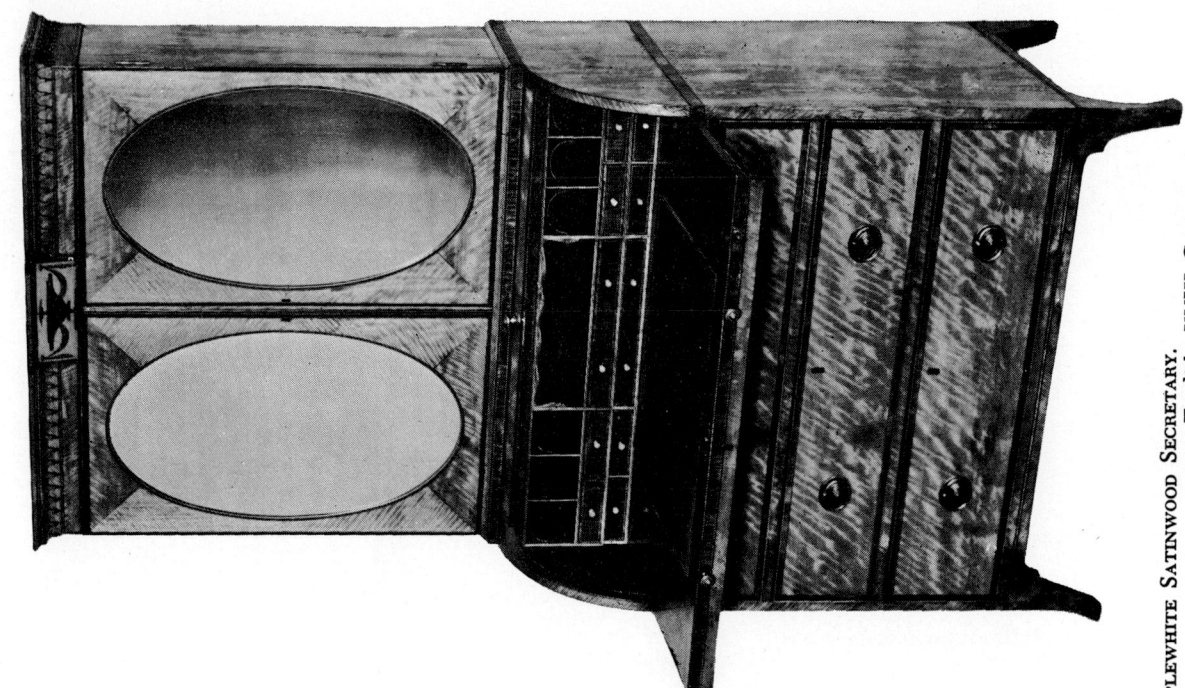

603. A Hepplewhite Mahogany Chest of Drawers.
English, XVIII Century

604. A Hepplewhite Satinwood Secretary.
English, XVIII Century
Courtesy of Needham's Antiques, Inc., New York City

605. A Mahogany Bookcase. With carved and inlaid pediment. English, XVIII Century

606. A Mahogany Secretary Bookcase.
English, XVIII Century
Courtesy of Needham's Antiques, Inc., New York City

ENGLISH FURNITURE 197

607. AN ADAM GILDED WALL MIRROR.
English, XVIII Century

608. AN ADAM GILDED WALL MIRROR.
English, XVIII Century

609. AN ADAM GILDED WALL SCONCE WITH
DRAPERY APPLIQUÉ.
English, XVIII Century

Florence H. Crane Collection.
Photograph by Taylor & Dull

610. A Sheraton Mahogany Armchair.   English, XVIII Century

611. A Sheraton Mahogany Side Chair.   English, XVIII Century

612. A Sheraton Mahogany Bergère.   English, XVIII Century

613. A Sheraton Mahogany Bergère.   English, XVIII Century

614. A Sheraton Mahogany Canterbury. English, circa 1800

615. A Sheraton Mahogany Waiter. English, circa 1800

616. A Sheraton Mahogany Work Table. An adaptation of a design by Thomas Sheraton, derived from a French model. English, circa 1800

617. A Sheraton Sycamore Envelope Table. English, XVIII Century

618. A Sheraton Mahogany Gaming and Writing Table. English, XVIII Century

619. A Sheraton Mahogany Occasional Table. English, XVIII Century

621. A Sheraton Mahogany Spider-Leg Table. Inlaid with a delicate linked and diced block-pattern banding. In common with certain other examples illustrated here, still open to proof as an additional Irish model.
British Isles, circa 1800

620. A George III Mahogany "Croft." With label of Seddon, Sons and Shackleton, giving an account of its uses. K. Barron lock, #268.
London, circa 1795-1800
*Florence H. Crane Collection.
Photograph by Taylor & Dull*

622. A Sheraton Mahogany Kidney-Shaped Table. British Isles, circa 1800

ENGLISH FURNITURE

624. A Sheraton Satinwood and Rosewood Sofa Table.
English, XVIII Century

623. A Sheraton Rosewood Sofa Table.
English, XVIII Century

A DIRECTORY OF ANTIQUE FURNITURE

625. A Sheraton Mahogany Writing Table.
English, XVIII Century

Robert J. Dunham Collection.
Photograph by Taylor & Dull

626. A Sheraton Mahogany Writing Table.
English, circa 1800

ENGLISH FURNITURE

627. A Sheraton Mahogany Drum Table.
English, XVIII Century

628. A George III Mahogany Rent Table.
English, XVIII Century
Florence H. Crane Collection.
Photograph by Taylor & Dull

631. A Sheraton Mahogany Side Table.
English, XVIII Century

629. A Sheraton Mahogany Console.
English, XVIII Century
Courtesy of Arthur S. Vernay, Inc., New York City

630. A Sheraton Satinwood Card Table.
English, circa 1800

ENGLISH FURNITURE

633. A Sheraton Mahogany Sideboard.
English, XVIII Century

632. A Sheraton Mahogany Sideboard.
English, XVIII Century

A DIRECTORY OF ANTIQUE FURNITURE

634. A Sheraton Mahogany Breakfast Table. English, XVIII Century

636. A Sheraton Mahogany Drop-Leaf Table. English, XVIII Century

635. A Sheraton Mahogany Breakfast Table. English, XVIII Century

ENGLISH FURNITURE

637. A GEORGE III MAHOGANY HORSESHOE DINING TABLE. A form shown by Thomas Shearer, and *The London Cabinet-Maker's Union Book of Prices.* English, XVIII Century

638. A SHERATON MAHOGANY PEDESTAL DINING TABLE. English, XVIII Century

639. A SHERATON MAHOGANY PEDESTAL DINING TABLE. English, XVIII Century

A DIRECTORY OF ANTIQUE FURNITURE

640. A Sheraton Mahogany Open-Shelf Console Table. English, circa 1800
Henry P. Strause Collection.
Photograph by Taylor & Dull

642. A Sheraton Mahogany Fiddle-Back Mahogany Chest of Drawers.
English, XVIII Century

641. A Sheraton Mahogany Butler's Chest with Drop Leaves. English, XVIII Century
Mrs. Dwight Davis Collection.
Photograph by Taylor & Dull

ENGLISH FURNITURE

643. A Sheraton Mahogany Secretary.
English, XVIII Century
Courtesy of Needham's Antiques, Inc., New York City

644. A Sheraton Mahogany Cabinet.
English, XVIII Century
Courtesy of Needham's Antiques, Inc., New York City

645. A Sheraton Mahogany Secretary Bookcase.
Courtesy of Needham's Antiques, Inc., New York City

English, XVIII Century

ENGLISH FURNITURE

648. A REGENCY MAHOGANY
ARMCHAIR.   English, circa 1810

647. A REGENCY MAHOGANY SIDE
CHAIR.   English, circa 1810

646. A GEORGE III GILDED AND
EBONIZED WALL SCONCE.
English, circa 1800

649. A REGENCY MAHOGANY SIDE
CHAIR.   English, circa 1810

650. A REGENCY MAHOGANY
ARMCHAIR.   English, circa 1810

651. A REGENCY MAHOGANY UPHOLSTERED ARMCHAIR.
English, circa 1810

654. A REGENCY MAHOGANY READING STAND.
English, circa 1810

653. A REGENCY MAHOGANY STRADDLE CHAIR.
British Isles, circa 1810

652. A REGENCY MAHOGANY LIBRARY ARMCHAIR. Opening as a set of steps.
English, circa 1810

655. A REGENCY ROSEWOOD TEAPOY.
English, circa 1810

656. A REGENCY MAHOGANY AND ORMOLU DAVENPORT.
English, circa 1820

ENGLISH FURNITURE 213

657. A Regency Mahogany Sofa Table.
English, circa 1800

658. A Regency Rosewood Sofa Table.
English, circa 1820

659. A Regency Satinwood Writing Table.
English, circa 1810

A DIRECTORY OF ANTIQUE FURNITURE

660. A REGENCY MAHOGANY LIBRARY TABLE. Mounted in ormolu; fitted with Bramah locks, the drawers constructed with grooved fillets.　　　　　　　English, circa 1810-1820

661. A REGENCY MAHOGANY HORSESHOE DESK.
English, circa 1810-1820

ENGLISH FURNITURE

663. A REGENCY ROSEWOOD BOOKSTAND.
English, Early XIX Century

662. A REGENCY MAHOGANY KNEEHOLE DESK.
English, circa 1820

665. A REGENCY MAHOGANY TRESTLE BOOKSTAND.
English, circa 1810

664. A REGENCY MAHOGANY REVOLVING BOOKSTAND.
English, circa 1815

666. A Regency Mahogany Card Table.
English, circa 1810

667. A Regency Mahogany Card Table.
English, circa 1810

668. A Regency Rosewood Card Table.
English, circa 1815

669. A Regency Rosewood and Mahogany Breakfast Table. English, circa 1810

ENGLISH FURNITURE

671. A Regency Rosewood and Buhlwork Commode. English, circa 1820

670. A Regency Mahogany Open-Shelf Cabinet. English, circa 1815

672. A Regency Mahogany Chest of Drawers. With evidences of circular sawing, and concentric-ringed screw heads.
English, circa 1820-1830

218 A DIRECTORY OF ANTIQUE FURNITURE

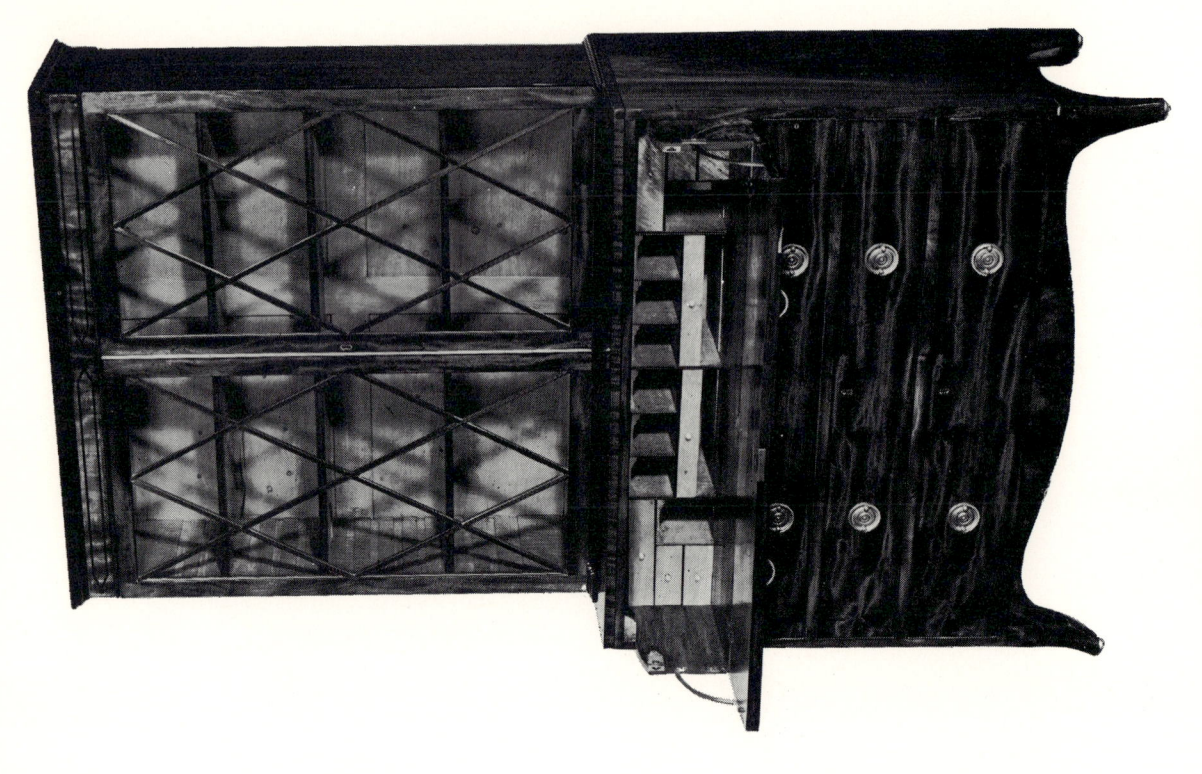

674. A Regency Mahogany Secretary.
English, circa 1810

673. A Regency Mahogany Chest-on-Chest.
English, circa 1810

675. A "Chippendale" Mahogany Bookcase. Inventoried in a Scottish collection circa 1835, not too long after its manufacture. English, Early XIX Century

676. A Regency Gilded Girandole Mirror. With original label of Thomas Fentham, London, who catered to an export business.
English, circa 1810

IRISH FURNITURE,
BASED ON ENGLISH AND CONTINENTAL DESIGNS

IRISH FURNITURE

677. A Walnut Twin-Chair-Back Settee.
Irish, XVIII Century

678. A Walnut Armchair.
Irish, XVIII Century

679. A Walnut Armchair. Related to Pennsylvania designs.
Irish, XVIII Century

680. A WALNUT SIDE TABLE. Regarded as Dutch by an auction expert.
Irish, XVIII Century

681. A WALNUT SIDE TABLE.
Irish, XVIII Century

682. A WALNUT SIDE TABLE. Inlaid with a shaded billet banding. Typical Dutch construction, but in ash and pine; regarded in Holland as very close to Dutch design.
Irish, XVIII Century

683. A YEWWOOD SIDE TABLE. A similar foot appears in New England work.
Welsh, XVIII Century

IRISH FURNITURE

684. A WALNUT KNEEHOLE COMMODE. Inlaid with a delicate shaded billet-chain banding.
Irish, XVIII Century

685. A WALNUT BUREAU. Compare the partition scrolls with Fig. 324.
Irish, XVIII Century

686. A WALNUT BUREAU.
Irish, XVIII Century

224 A DIRECTORY OF ANTIQUE FURNITURE

688. A Walnut Chest-on-Chest.
Irish or Welsh, XVIII Century

687. A Walnut Chest-on-Chest.
Irish, XVIII Century

IRISH FURNITURE

689. A WALNUT SECRETARY. With Dutch type cockbead drawer surrounds, the entire design accepted as Dutch by authority in Holland. Possibly executed in Ireland. The feet are replacements.
Dutch School, XVIII Century

A DIRECTORY OF ANTIQUE FURNITURE

691. A Walnut Side Chair. Irish, XVIII Century

690. A Walnut Side Chair. Irish chair-makers often employed cabriole legs with all feet carved and matching, a habit which has come to be regarded as a rare feature of English working method. Irish, XVIII Century

692. A Walnut and Mahogany Armchair. Irish, XVIII Century

694. A Mahogany Twin-Chair-Back Settee. This type of arm terminal was transmitted to Scandinavia. Irish, XVIII Century

693. A Mahogany Side Chair. Irish, XVIII Century

695. A Walnut Armchair. The design of the arm support recently claimed for Southern states here. Irish, XVIII Century

IRISH FURNITURE

697. A Walnut Stretcher Chair. The arms have been removed. Similar stretchers employed in Philadelphia and Newport.
Irish, XVIII Century

696. A Mahogany Side Chair.
Irish, XVIII Century

698. A Walnut Side Chair.
Irish, XVIII Century

700. A Walnut Side Chair. The stretcher associated with Philadelphia designs. Irish, XVIII Century

699. A Walnut Armchair. Variations of this model, and others illustrated here, sometimes appear with eagle-head arm terminals.
Irish, XVIII Century

701. A Mahogany Armchair. The whorled roll terminal, projecting behind the splat, is sometimes considered a rare feature of English design. Irish, XVIII Century

A DIRECTORY OF ANTIQUE FURNITURE

702. A MAHOGANY ARMCHAIR.
Irish, XVIII Century

703. A MAHOGANY STRADDLE CHAIR.
Irish, XVIII Century

704. A WALNUT FAN-BACK SIDE CHAIR. Regarded as North German by an auction expert!
Irish, XVIII Century

705. A MAHOGANY TWIN-CHAIR-BACK SETTEE. The shape and piercing of the splat followed in America.
Irish, XVIII Century

706. A MAHOGANY WHEEL-BACK ARMCHAIR. Irish, XVIII Century

707. A MAHOGANY ARMCHAIR. The splat related to Philadelphia designs.
Irish, XVIII Century

708. A WALNUT ARMCHAIR. Versions of the tasseled drapery splat are found in New England and Pennsylvania.
Irish, XVIII Century

IRISH FURNITURE

710. A Mahogany Twin-Chair-Back Settee. Said to have been made in America according to "designs and specifications" brought over from Chippendale's shop!
Irish design and Irish work, XVIII Century

712. A Walnut Side Chair.
Irish, XVIII Century

711. A Mahogany Side Chair.
Irish, XVIII Century

709. A Mahogany Corner Chair.
Irish, XVIII Century

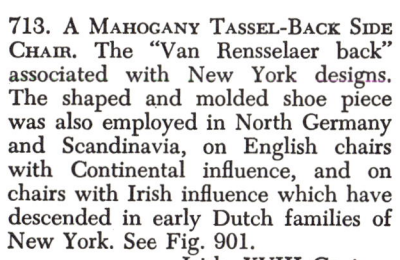

713. A Mahogany Tassel-Back Side Chair. The "Van Rensselaer back" associated with New York designs. The shaped and molded shoe piece was also employed in North Germany and Scandinavia, on English chairs with Continental influence, and on chairs with Irish influence which have descended in early Dutch families of New York. See Fig. 901.
Irish, XVIII Century

714. A Mahogany Corner Chair.
Irish, XVIII Century

A DIRECTORY OF ANTIQUE FURNITURE

716. A Mahogany Corner Chair.
Irish, XVIII Century

715. A Walnut Side Chair.
Irish, XVIII Century

717. A Mahogany Corner Chair. The splat and posts followed in American designs. Irish, XVIII Century

720. A Mahogany Side Chair. The frilled crest also featured in New York chairs. Irish, XVIII Century

718. A Mahogany Armchair. With eagle-head arm terminals. Irish, XVIII Century

719. A Mahogany Side Chair.
Irish, XVIII Century

721. A Mahogany Armchair.
Irish, XVIII Century

IRISH FURNITURE

722. A Mahogany Side Chair. Similar designs are found in Denmark.
Irish, XVIII Century

723. A Mahogany Armchair. Similar splat designs appear in examples received into German and Scandinavian collections of long standing, some with open bar seat braces.
Irish, XVIII Century

724. A Mahogany Armchair.
Irish, XVIII Century

725. A Mahogany Armchair. The "Chippendale" back here combined with cabriole legs of earlier type.
Irish, XVIII Century

726. A Mahogany Side Chair.
Irish, XVIII Century

727. A Mahogany Side Chair.
Irish, XVIII Century

728. A Mahogany Side Chair.
Irish, XVIII Century

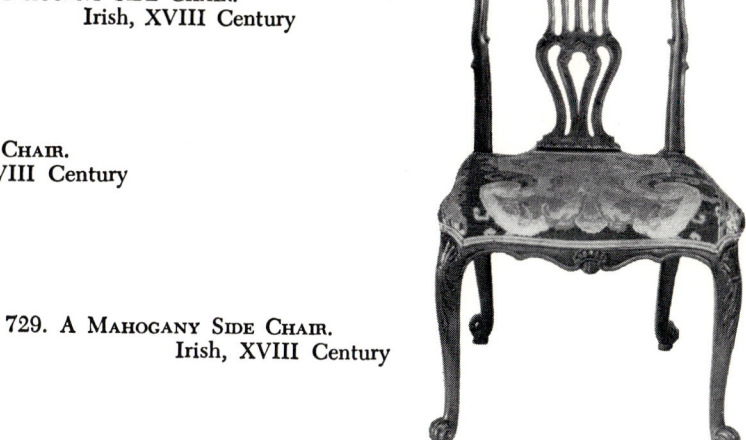

729. A Mahogany Side Chair.
Irish, XVIII Century

730. A Mahogany Upholstered Armchair.   Irish, XVIII Century

733. A Mahogany Love Seat.   Irish, XVIII Century

734. A Mahogany Love Seat.   Irish, XVIII Century

731. A Mahogany Upholstered Armchair.   Irish, XVIII Century

IRISH FURNITURE

732. A Mahogany Upholstered
Open-Arm Easy Chair.
Irish, XVIII Century

735. A Mahogany Upholstered
Armchair.   Irish, XVIII Century

738. A Mahogany Upholstered
Side Chair.   Irish, XVIII Century

737. A Mahogany Upholstered
Armchair.   Irish, XVIII Century

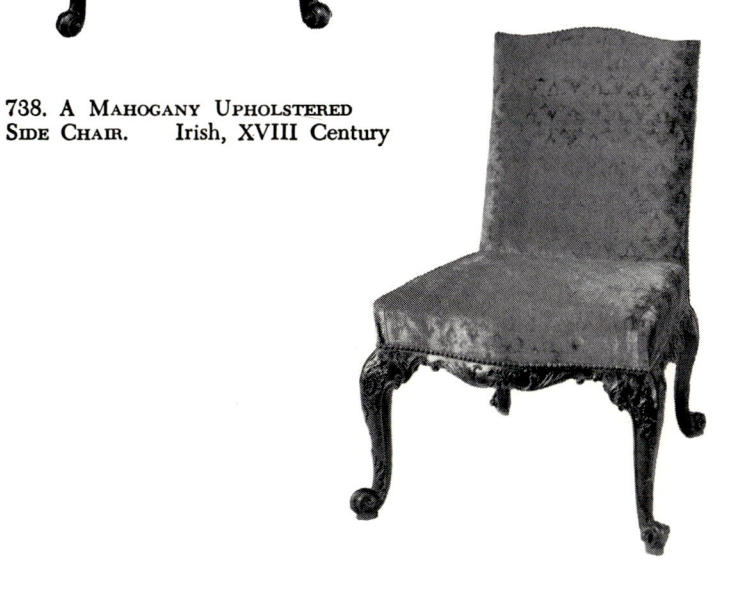

739. A Mahogany Upholstered
Side Chair.   Irish, XVIII Century

736. A Mahogany Upholstered Armchair. Irish, XVIII Century

740. A Mahogany Upholstered Armchair. Irish, XVIII Century

741. A Mahogany Upholstered Settee. Irish, XVIII Century

IRISH FURNITURE

742. A Mahogany Basin Stand.
Irish, XVIII Century

743. A Mahogany Tripod Table.
Irish, XVIII Century

747. A Mahogany Tripod Stand.
Irish, XVIII Century

744. A Mahogany Tripod Table.
Irish, XVIII Century

749. A Mahogany Dumbwaiter.
Irish, XVIII Century

748. A Mahogany Tilting-Top Tripod Table. With typical "bird cage" platform. Considered in Holland as probably by a Dutch craftsman ... working in that country or Ireland. Related to Philadelphia designs.
Irish, XVIII Century

745. A Mahogany Tilting-Top Tripod Table.
Irish, XVIII Century

746. A Mahogany Tilting-Top Tripod Table.
Irish, XVIII Century

751. A Mahogany Tray-Top Table.
Irish, XVIII Century

753. A Mahogany Drop-Leaf
Table.   Irish, XVIII Century

752. A Mahogany Writing Table. Very late eighteenth century work, with "Sheraton pink" interior staining wash.
Irish, XVIII Century

750. A Mahogany Drop-Leaf
Table.   Irish, XVIII Century

A DIRECTORY OF ANTIQUE FURNITURE

754. A Mahogany Card Table.
Irish, XVIII Century

755. A Mahogany Card Table.
Irish, XVIII Century

756. A Walnut Card Table.
Irish, XVIII Century

IRISH FURNITURE

239

757. A Walnut Card Table.
Irish, XVIII Century

758. A Mahogany Card Table.
Irish, XVIII Century

759. A Mahogany Card Table.
Irish, XVIII Century

760. A MAHOGANY CARD TABLE. With pulvinar frieze, as found in a number of larger side tables in American collections, believed to be of Philadelphia origin.   Irish, XVIII Century
Courtesy of M. Harris & Sons, London

IRISH FURNITURE

761. A Mahogany Side Table.
Irish, XVIII Century

762. A Mahogany Side Table.
Irish, XVIII Century

764. A Mahogany Commode. The stiles and base similar to these features of the Leverhulme cabinet referred to; this cabinet additionally ornamented with *espagnolette* capitals and buhlwork. Irish, Late XVIII Century

763. A Rosewood Commode. With "open-mouth" escutcheons as commonly found in Sweden. The handles matching those of a very fine Georgian-Louis XIV cabinet lately discovered in London, related to an example in the Leverhulme Collection when this was dispersed in New York City. Walnut drawer linings. Irish, XVIII Century

IRISH FURNITURE

765. A Mahogany Kneehole Desk. Regarded in Holland as possibly of Dutch craftsmanship.
Irish, XVIII Century

766. A Mahogany Bureau. With finest London-type construction in oak and pine, the drawer partitions of full depth.
Irish, XVIII Century
Courtesy of J. J. Wolff (Antiques) Ltd., New York City
Photograph by Taylor & Dull

768. A Mahogany Secretary. Described as Dutch or Westphalian. Irish, XVIII Century

767. An Oak and Mahogany Bureau. Inlaid with a delicate shaded billet-chain banding, the bird and stellate inlays similar to German work, and to Irish Hepplewhite designs; oak and pine construction. Irish, XVIII Century

IRISH FURNITURE 245

769. A Parcel-Gilded Walnut Cabinet. The inside surfaces of the cupboard doors faced with patterned veneers, in the German manner. Similar carved astragal patterns appear in equally fine Irish mahogany examples of Chippendale designs.
Irish, XVIII Century

770. A Mahogany Secretary. With finely carved, paneled, and fitted interior sections. This type of Irish foot sometimes replaced.
Irish, XVIII Century
Courtesy of Needham's Antiques, Inc., New York City

246 A DIRECTORY OF ANTIQUE FURNITURE

771. A Mahogany Secretary. With pedimental cartouche favored in Philadelphia, and "drip" cornice member; the quarter-round base molding and ogee feet are also characteristic.
Irish, XVIII Century

772. A Mahogany Secretary.
Irish, XVIII Century

773. A Mahogany Bookcase. With central pull-out writing table, and numerous masked drawers in the brieze and below.
Irish, XVIII Century

774. A Mahogany Side Chair.
Irish, XVIII Century

775. A Mahogany Side Chair.
Irish, XVIII Century

776. A Mahogany Upholstered Armchair. Irish, XVIII Century

777. A Mahogany Upholstered Armchair. Irish, XVIII Century

IRISH FURNITURE

778. A Mahogany Upholstered Armchair.   Irish, XVIII Century

779. A Mahogany Upholstered Armchair.   Irish, XVIII Century
Courtesy of J. J. Wolff (Antiques) Ltd., New York City

780. A Mahogany Upholstered Settee.   Irish, XVIII Century

A DIRECTORY OF ANTIQUE FURNITURE

781. A Mahogany Twin-Chair-Back Settee. Related to Philadelphia designs. Irish, XVIII Century

782. A Mahogany Twin-Chair-Back Settee. Irish, XVIII Century

783. A Mahogany Twin-Chair-Back Settee. Irish, XVIII Century

IRISH FURNITURE

784. A Mahogany Side Chair. The leg design has recently been claimed for Southern states here.
Irish, XVIII Century

789. A Mahogany Twin-Chair-Back Settee. A side chair of marked similarity is exhibited in the Flensburg Museum, Denmark, apparently copied from an Irish model.
Irish, XVIII Century

788. A Mahogany Side Chair.
Irish or Welsh, XVIII Century

787. A Mahogany Armchair.
Irish, XVIII Century
*Victoria & Albert Museum.
Crown Copyright.*

785. A Mahogany Side Chair.
Irish, XVIII Century

786. A Mahogany Armchair.
Irish, XVIII Century

A DIRECTORY OF ANTIQUE FURNITURE

793. A Mahogany Side Chair.
Irish, XVIII Century

792. A Mahogany Side Chair.
Irish, XVIII Century

791. A Mahogany Armchair. Related to Philadelphia designs. See Fig. 228. Irish, XVIII Century
Courtesy of Needham's Antiques, Inc., New York City

795. A Mahogany Side Chair. A number of slightly finer examples with this type of splat appear in German collections, usually ascribed to Dessau, capital of Anhalt-Dessau, circa 1800.
Irish, XVIII Century

794. A Mahogany Armchair.
Irish, XVIII Century

790. A Mahogany Chair-Back Settee. The leaf carving no bolder than shown in Chippendale's design with this splat. Similar splats appear in Hamburg chairs.
Irish, XVIII Century

IRISH FURNITURE

796.

797.

798.

796. A Walnut Armchair. See Fig. 261. Irish, XVIII Century

797. A Mahogany Armchair. A correct version of Irish Chippendale design. Irish, XVIII Century

798. A Mahogany Side Chair. Irish, XVIII Century

799. A Mahogany Side Chair. Irish, XVIII Century

800. A Mahogany Side Chair. Irish, XVIII Century

801. A Mahogany Side Chair. Regarded as Hanoverian by an auction expert. Irish, XVIII Century

802. A Mahogany Side Chair. The front and side rails in ash, faced with mahogany. Rear feet characteristic of Dublin, Hamburg and Altona. Irish, Late XVIII Century

803. A Mahogany Side Chair. Irish, XVIII Century

799.

801.

802.

800.

803.

A DIRECTORY OF ANTIQUE FURNITURE

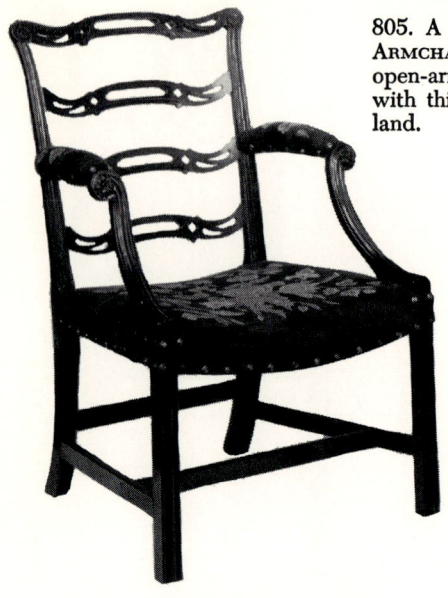

805. A Mahogany Ladder-Back Armchair. Very fine upholstered open-arm easy chairs were made, with this type of arm support, in Ireland. *Irish, XVIII Century*

806. A Mahogany Ladder-Back Armchair. *Irish, XVIII Century*

807. A Mahogany Ladder-Back Armchair. *Irish, XVIII Century*

804. A Walnut Side Chair. The design of the splat appearing in one example attributed to James Gillingham of Philadelphia. *Irish, circa 1800*

808. A Cherrywood Upholstered Armchair. This design calls for simple "C" brackets (missing here) at the front legs, similar to Fig. 791. *Irish, XVIII Century*

809. A Mahogany Upholstered Settee. Related to Philadelphia designs. Similar models were made with solid leg brackets, narrow, and running horizontally, with ogee stops. *Irish, XVIII Century*

IRISH FURNITURE

810. A "George II" Mahogany Cellaret. Representing a principal misunderstanding of Irish furniture . . . to a practical eye, unfettered by English developments, the actual age of this example coincides with the Sheraton-Regency period, rather than its published date of "c. 1740."

Irish, circa 1800-1810

811. A Mahogany Silver Table. A related example expertized as American and sold here at five thousand dollars.   *Irish, XVIII Century*

812. A Mahogany Drop-Leaf Table.   *Irish, XVIII Century*

814. A Mahogany Side Table.
Irish, XVIII Century

813. A Mahogany Drawing Table.
Irish, XVIII Century

815. A Mahogany Card Table.
Irish, XVIII Century

IRISH FURNITURE

816. A Mahogany Card Table.
Irish, XVIII Century

817. A Mahogany Card Table.
From Portsmouth, New Hampshire.
Irish, XVIII Century

A DIRECTORY OF ANTIQUE FURNITURE

818. A MAHOGANY KNEEHOLE COMMODE. One of many pieces coupled with names of English collectors, and addresses, but strongly indicative of Irish work in design, minor structural techniques, or late execution.
British Isles, XVIII Century

819. A MAHOGANY BUREAU. Inlaid with a delicate open billet-chain banding. Oak and pine construction, with "Sheraton pink" staining wash.
Irish, XVIII Century

IRISH FURNITURE

820. A MAHOGANY SECRETARY. With typical English construction, and full-length drawer partitions in pine, the shaped small drawers lined with cedar; secret compartments in the central cupboard section. Irish, XVIII Century
Courtesy of Courtright House, Inc., Boston, Mass.

822. A Mahogany Cabinet. Much finer examples were produced in Ireland with this type of stile, and cornice. Related to designs in Holstein and Lubeck. See Fig. 278. Irish, XVIII Century

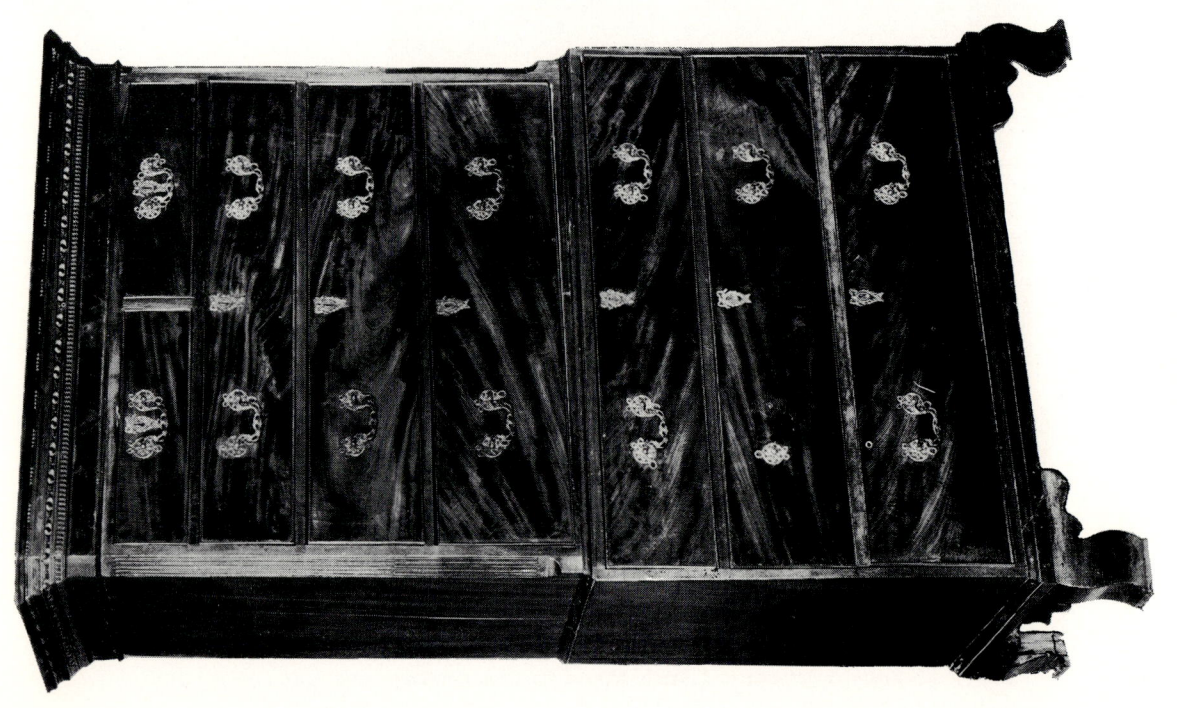

821. A Mahogany Chest-on-Chest. Irish, XVIII Century

IRISH FURNITURE

824. A "William Kent" Mahogany Corner Cabinet. Related to designs in Schleswig-Holstein and Lubeck.
Irish, XVIII Century

823. A Mahogany Secretary. Sheraton period work, with oak, walnut and pine secondary woods. Restoration includes reshaping of the feet. The fretted cornice and frieze similar to work in Charleston, South Carolina.
Irish, XVIII Century

825. A Gilded Overmantel Mirror.
Irish, XVIII Century

826. A Gilded Wall Mirror.
Irish, XVIII Century

827. A Gilded Wall Mirror.
Irish, XVIII Century

IRISH FURNITURE

828. A GILDED WALL MIRROR. Similar designs have been ascribed to Philadelphia. Irish, XVIII Century

829. A GILDED WALL MIRROR.
Irish, XVIII Century

830. A GILDED WALL MIRROR.
Irish, XVIII Century

831. A GILDED WALL MIRROR. Regarded as an Early Georgian design, the recurved pediment centers a basket of flowers and *wheat ears*.
Irish, XVIII Century

832. A PARCEL-GILDED MAHOGANY GIRANDOLE MIRROR. The Metropolitan and Winterthur Museums exhibit similar mirrors as of American origin.
Irish, XVIII Century

834. A PARCEL-GILDED WALNUT WALL MIRROR.
Irish, XVIII Century

833. A PARCEL-GILDED WALNUT GIRANDOLE MIRROR.
Irish, XVIII Century
Courtesy of J. J. Wolff (Antiques) Ltd., New York City

IRISH FURNITURE

835. A Parcel-Gilded Walnut "Constitution" Mirror.
Irish, XVIII Century

836. A Parcel-Gilded Mahogany Wall Mirror. A type which appears with the so-called "Philadelphia urn" finial. The delicate open spiry stems of the side pendants, and eagle heads in heraldic regardant attitude, appear in Irish designs.
British Isles, XVIII Century

840. A Parcel-Gilded Walnut Wall Mirror. The urn finial associated with more sophisticated Hepplewhite designs.
Irish, Late XVIII Century

837. A Parcel-Gilded Mahogany Wall Mirror. With side pendants resembling those of the two preceding examples, and typical Irish valanced base. Irish, XVIII Century

838. A Parcel-Gilded Walnut Wall Mirror.
Irish, XVIII Century
Courtesy of J. J. Wolff (Antiques) Ltd., New York City

839. A Parcel-Gilded Walnut Wall Mirror.
Irish, XVIII Century

841. A Mahogany Upholstered Armchair.   Irish, XVIII Century

842. A Mahogany Upholstered Armchair.   Irish, XVIII Century

843. A Mahogany Window Seat.
Irish, XVIII Century

844. A Mahogany Upholstered Settee.   Irish, XVIII Century

IRISH FURNITURE

846. A Mahogany Armchair.
Irish, XVIII Century

845. A Mahogany Wheel-Back Armchair. Apparently made by a Continental (German) craftsman in Ireland.
British Isles, XVIII Century

847. A Mahogany Side Chair. Related to Baltimore designs.
Irish, XVIII Century

848. A Mahogany Armchair.
Irish, XVIII Century

849. A Mahogany Armchair.
Irish, XVIII Century

850. A Mahogany Side Chair.
Irish, XVIII Century

A DIRECTORY OF ANTIQUE FURNITURE

853. A Mahogany Card Table.
Irish, XVIII Century

851. A Mahogany Card Table.
Irish, XVIII Century

852. A Mahogany Card Table.
Irish, XVIII Century

IRISH FURNITURE

269

854. A Mahogany Pembroke Table.
Irish, XVIII Century

856. A Mahogany Console Card
Table. Irish, XVIII Century

855. A Satinwood Center Table.
Regarded as Continental by English
experts, but representative of such
work carried out in Ireland. Centered
keyholes in square locks.
Irish, circa 1800

857. A Sycamore Console Table.
William Moore, Dublin, circa 1785

858. A Sycamore Console Table.
William Moore, Dublin, circa 1785
Courtesy of Needham's Antiques, Inc., New York City

859. A Mahogany Side Table.
Irish, XVIII Century

860. A Mahogany Side Table.
Irish, XVIII Century

A DIRECTORY OF ANTIQUE FURNITURE

862. A Sycamore Corner Commode.
William Moore, Dublin, circa 1785

871. Sycamore and Mahogany
Hanging Shelves.
Irish, XVIII Century

863. A SYCAMORE MARQUETRY COMMODE. Widely shown and praised as a fine example of English cabinetwork.

William Moore, Dublin, circa 1785

Victoria & Albert Museum. Crown Copyright.

274 A DIRECTORY OF ANTIQUE FURNITURE

861. A Marquetry Commode.
Irish, XVIII Century

864. A Sycamore Marquetry
Cabinet.   Irish, XVIII Century
Courtesy of the Cooper Union Museum, New York City

865. A Mahogany Secretary. Oak and pine construction of English type, except that the drawer bottoms run from front to rear.
Irish, XVIII Century

866. A Mahogany Secretary. The pediment similar to Baltimore designs.
Irish, XVIII Century

867. A "HEPPLEWHITE INLAID SATINWOOD SECRETARY." Described as of Philadelphia or Baltimore origin, despite the design and use of knotty pine. At this time Philadelphia was shipping pine to Ireland, and glass!
Irish, XVIII Century

868. A MAHOGANY AND FRUITWOOD SECRETARY. Irish, XVIII Century

IRISH FURNITURE

869. A "Satinwood" Secretary. At this period fine cuttings of birch and fruitwoods, then popular on the Continent, were introduced in Great Britain, and, along with holly veneers, were used as substitutes for satinwood.
Irish, circa 1800

870. A "Satinwood" Secretary. With walnut, oak and pine secondary woods. Original handles; lever locks.
Irish, circa 1810

A DIRECTORY OF ANTIQUE FURNITURE

873. A MAHOGANY CARD TABLE.
Scottish, Late XVIII Century

872. A MAHOGANY SOFA TABLE. Scottish furniture joined other British exports to America at the close of the eighteenth century.
Scottish, XVIII Century

874. A MAHOGANY CHEST OF DRAWERS.
Scottish, Late XVIII Century

IRISH FURNITURE 279

875. A MAHOGANY CORNER CABINET.
Scottish, Late XVIII Century
Courtesy of Needham's Antiques, Inc., New York City

876. A MAHOGANY CORNER CABINET.
Scottish, Late XVIII Century
Courtesy of Needham's Antiques, Inc., New York City

877. A MAHOGANY SECRETARY. The urn-shaped astragals apparently taken from *The London Cabinet-Makers' Union Book of Prices.*
British Isles, circa 1810

878. A Mahogany Breakfront Bookcase.   Scottish, circa 1800

878A. A Marble Mantel in the Adam Style, with Bossi Inlays.
Irish, circa 1785
Courtesy of Pratt & Son, Ltd., London

AMERICAN FURNITURE, BASED ON ENGLISH AND IRISH DESIGNS

879. A Walnut Wainscot Armchair. Pennsylvania, XVII-XVIII Century
J. Stogdell Stokes Collection.
Photograph by Taylor & Dull

880. A Spirally-Turned Oak Side Chair. New Jersey, circa 1700
J. Stogdell Stokes Collection.
Photograph by Taylor & Dull

AMERICAN FURNITURE

881. A WALNUT SIDE CHAIR.
   New England, XVIII Century

882. A WALNUT SIDE CHAIR.
   New England, XVIII Century

883. A WALNUT SIDE CHAIR.
   New England, XVIII Century
Marsden J. Perry Collection.
Photograph by Taylor & Dull

884. A WALNUT ARMCHAIR.
   Philadelphia, XVIII Century

885. A Mahogany Side Chair. The finely grained splat shaped out of solid mahogany.
Philadelphia, XVIII Century
Norvin H. Green Collection.
Photograph by Taylor & Dull

887. A Mahogany Armchair. Compare the arm support with Figs. 695 and 702.
Philadelphia, XVIII Century

886. A Mahogany Side Chair. Similar examples appear with eagle-head arm terminals.
New York, XVIII Century
Norvin H. Green Collection.
Photograph by Taylor & Dull

888. A Mahogany Armchair.
Philadelphia, XVIII Century

890. A Walnut Side Chair.
Philadelphia, XVIII Century

889. A Mahogany Armchair.
Philadelphia, XVIII Century

AMERICAN FURNITURE

285

891. A WALNUT SIDE CHAIR.
Philadelphia, XVIII Century

892. A MAHOGANY SIDE CHAIR.
Philadelphia, XVIII Century

893. A WALNUT ARMCHAIR. With Irish-type splat.
Pennsylvania, XVIII Century
Norvin H. Green Collection.
Photograph by Taylor & Dull

894. A CHERRYWOOD SIDE CHAIR.
Eliphalet Chapin, East Windsor, Conn., XVIII Century
Norvin H. Green Collection.
Photograph by Taylor & Dull

895. A MAHOGANY SIDE CHAIR. Recorded as formerly owned by General Anthony Wayne.
Philadelphia, XVIII Century

896. A MAHOGANY SIDE CHAIR.
Philadelphia, XVIII Century

A DIRECTORY OF ANTIQUE FURNITURE

897. A MAHOGANY SIDE CHAIR. The vertical carving above the knee is characteristic of Irish designs.
Philadelphia, XVIII Century
Norvin H. Green Collection.
Photograph by Taylor & Dull

898. A MAHOGANY SIDE CHAIR.
Philadelphia, XVIII Century

899. A WALNUT SIDE CHAIR. Compare these, and other cabriole legs here, with Figs. 713-714.
Philadelphia, XVIII Century
George M. Curtis Collection
Photograph by Taylor & Dull

900. A MAHOGANY SIDE CHAIR. The deep scroll of the knee is a typical feature of Irish design, appearing here in one of the finest examples of Philadelphia craftsmanship.
Philadelphia, XVIII Century

901. A MAHOGANY SIDE CHAIR. A matching armchair, from the Metropolitan Museum of Art, has been published as illustrating the progression from earlier Dutch influence to the English Chippendale mode. Actually, earlier Irish influence is continued here, in another Irish model, not English, and having no relation to Chippendale's designs.
New York, XVIII Century
Norvin H. Green Collection.
Photograph by Taylor & Dull

902. A MAHOGANY SIDE CHAIR.
Philadelphia, XVIII Century

AMERICAN FURNITURE

906. A Mahogany Corner Chair.
Described as English!
New York, XVIII Century

903. A Mahogany Side Chair. Recorded as formerly owned by President Willard of Harvard College.
New England, XVIII Century
George M. Curtis Collection.
Photograph by Taylor & Dull

904. A Mahogany Armchair.
Massachusetts, XVIII Century
Norvin H. Green Collection.
Photograph by Taylor & Dull

905. A Mahogany Side Chair.
Massachusetts, XVIII Century
Ralph Blum Collection.
Photograph by Taylor & Dull

907. A Mahogany Side Chair.
New York, XVIII Century

908. A Mahogany Side Chair.
New York, XVIII Century

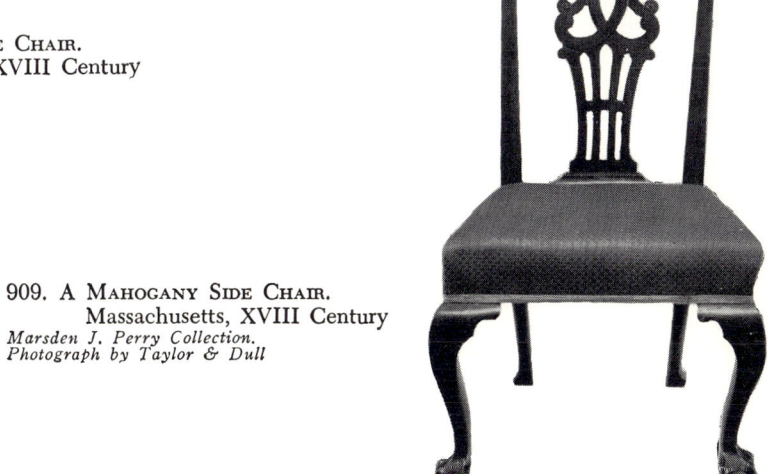

909. A Mahogany Side Chair.
Massachusetts, XVIII Century
Marsden J. Perry Collection.
Photograph by Taylor & Dull

A DIRECTORY OF ANTIQUE FURNITURE

910. A MAHOGANY SIDE CHAIR. With typical Irish splat; compare Fig. 785.
Massachusetts, XVIII Century

912. A MAHOGANY SIDE CHAIR. The downward scroll of the leaf motives carved upon the knees is an Irish impropriety.
Philadelphia, XVIII Century
*Ralph Blum Collection.
Photograph by Taylor & Dull*

911. A MAHOGANY SIDE CHAIR.
Massachusetts, XVIII Century

914. A MAHOGANY SIDE CHAIR. With features of design and carved details indicating the presence of Irish craftsmen in the finest shops of Philadelphia.
Philadelphia, XVIII Century
Courtesy of Joe Kindig, Jr. & Son, York, Pennsylvania

913. A MAHOGANY SIDE CHAIR.
Philadelphia, XVIII Century

915. A MAHOGANY SIDE CHAIR. Also of outstanding quality; compare the splat with Figs. 543 and 791.
Philadelphia, XVIII Century

AMERICAN FURNITURE

916. A CHIPPENDALE MAHOGANY SIDE CHAIR.
Philadelphia, XVIII Century

918. A CHIPPENDALE MAHOGANY LADDER-BACK SIDE CHAIR.
Philadelphia, XVIII Century

917. A CHIPPENDALE MAHOGANY SIDE CHAIR.
Philadelphia, XVIII Century

925. A PAINTED WINDSOR ARMCHAIR.
Pennsylvania, XVIII Century

919. A CHIPPENDALE MAHOGANY LADDER-BACK SIDE CHAIR.
Philadelphia, XVIII Century

924. A BRACE-BACK WINDSOR ARMCHAIR.
New England, XVIII Century

920. A Hickory and Maple Windsor Armchair.
  Pennsylvania, XVIII Century
J. Stogdell Stokes Collection.
Photograph by Taylor & Dull

921. An Oak, Hickory and Maple Windsor Armchair.
  By Richmond of Philadelphia,
  XVIII Century
J. Stogdell Stokes Collection.
Photograph by Taylor & Dull

926. A Hickory, Maple and Walnut Windsor Writing Armchair.
  By Richmond of Philadelphia,
  XVIII Century
J. Stogdell Stokes Collection.
Photograph by Taylor & Dull

922. A Maple and Hickory "Three-Back" Windsor Armchair.
  New England, XVIII Century
J. Stogdell Stokes Collection.
Photograph by Taylor & Dull

923. A Hickory and Maple Lady's Windsor Armchair.
  Cape Cod, XVIII Century
J. Stogdell Stokes Collection.
Photograph by Taylor & Dull

AMERICAN FURNITURE

927. A HEPPLEWHITE MAHOGANY SIDE CHAIR.
Baltimore, XVIII Century

928. A HEPPLEWHITE MAHOGANY ARMCHAIR.
Connecticut, XVIII Century
Norvin H. Green Collection.
Photograph by Taylor & Dull

929. A HEPPLEWHITE MAHOGANY SIDE CHAIR. New York, XVIII Century

930. A HEPPLEWHITE MAHOGANY SIDE CHAIR. American, XVIII Century

931. A HEPPLEWHITE MAHOGANY SIDE CHAIR. American, XVIII Century

932. A HEPPLEWHITE MAHOGANY SIDE CHAIR.
New England, XVIII Century

933. A HEPPLEWHITE MAHOGANY SIDE CHAIR.
New England, XVIII Century
Courtesy of Joe Kindig, Jr. & Son, York, Pennsylvania

934. A HEPPLEWHITE MAHOGANY SIDE CHAIR.
Massachusetts, XVIII Century

935. A HEPPLEWHITE MAHOGANY SIDE CHAIR.
New York, XVIII Century
*William Few Chrystie Collection.
Photograph by Taylor & Dull*

936. A HEPPLEWHITE MAHOGANY SIDE CHAIR.
American, XVIII Century

AMERICAN FURNITURE

938. A MAHOGANY SIDE CHAIR.
   New York City, circa 1800

939. A SHERATON MAHOGANY
ARMCHAIR.   New York City,
   Early XIX Century

937. A MAHOGANY SIDE CHAIR.
   American, circa 1800

940. A Duncan Phyfe Mahogany Side Chair.
New York City, circa 1805
William Few Chrystie Collection.
Photograph by Taylor & Dull

941. A Duncan Phyfe Mahogany Side Chair.
New York City, circa 1810

942. A Duncan Phyfe Mahogany Armchair.
New York City, circa 1815

943. A Duncan Phyfe Mahogany Side Chair.
New York City, circa 1820

944. A Duncan Phyfe Mahogany Side Chair.
New York City, circa 1820

AMERICAN FURNITURE

946. A WALNUT UPHOLSTERED ARMCHAIR.
American, XVIII Century
Norvin H. Green Collection.
Photograph by Taylor & Dull

947. A MAHOGANY UPHOLSTERED ARMCHAIR. Published comments, intended to reflect upon this rare frame, only indicated a want of knowledge on the part of "experts" unable to recognize a thoroughly genuine example when it appeared in the dispersal of an old collection. The foot is carved in an exactly similar manner to that of Benjamin Frothingham, Charleston, Mass., while the design shows a retention of the so-called "Chippendale" mode in this country for some years after the Revolution. New England, XVIII Century
Courtesy of Joe Kindig, Jr. & Son, York, Pennsylvania

296 A DIRECTORY OF ANTIQUE FURNITURE

949. A Mahogany Wing Chair.
American, XVIII Century

945. A Walnut Wing Chair.
American, XVIII Century

948. A Walnut Wing Chair.
American, XVIII Century
Norvin H. Green Collection.
Photograph by Taylor & Dull

AMERICAN FURNITURE

951. A MAHOGANY MARTHA
WASHINGTON ARMCHAIR.
New England, XVIII Century

952. A MAHOGANY MARTHA
WASHINGTON ARMCHAIR. One of a
rare pair.
New England, XVIII Century

950. A CHIPPENDALE CHERRYWOOD
WING CHAIR.
American, XVIII Century

A DIRECTORY OF ANTIQUE FURNITURE

953. AN INLAID MAHOGANY MARTHA WASHINGTON ARMCHAIR. With label of Joseph Short.
Newburyport, Mass., circa 1800

954. A HEPPLEWHITE MAHOGANY WING CHAIR.
American, XVIII Century

955. A MAHOGANY MARTHA WASHINGTON ARMCHAIR.
Salem, Mass., circa 1800
Norvin H. Green Collection.
Photograph by Taylor & Dull

AMERICAN FURNITURE

299

956. A Hepplewhite Mahogany Upholstered Settee.
American, XVIII Century

957. A Hepplewhite Mahogany Upholstered Settee.
American, XVIII Century
Courtesy of Joe Kindig, Jr. & Son, York, Pennsylvania

958. A Hepplewhite Mahogany Upholstered Settee.
American, XVIII Century

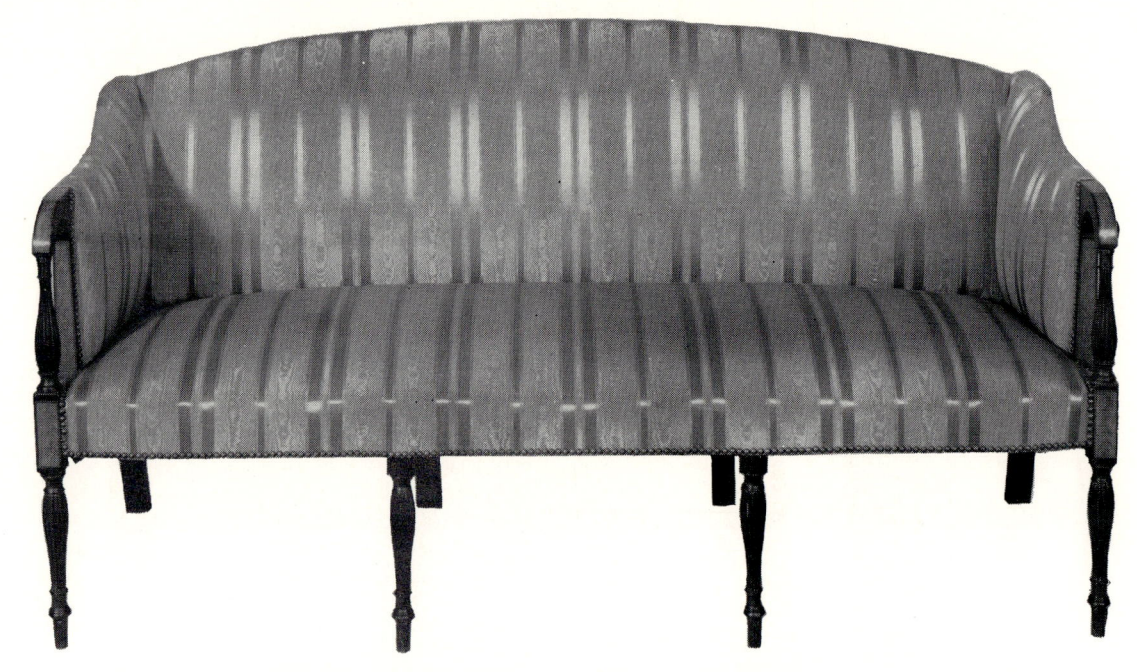

959. A Sheraton Mahogany and Branch Satinwood Settee. New England, circa 1800

962. A Duncan Phyfe Mahogany Settee. New York City, circa 1810

Norvin H. Green Collection.
Photograph by Taylor & Dull

961. A Duncan Phyfe Mahogany Settee. New York City, circa 1810

AMERICAN FURNITURE

960. A DUNCAN PHYFE MAHOGANY "RECAMIER" SOFA.
New York City, circa 1810

Norvin H. Green Collection.
Photograph by Taylor & Dull

963. A MAHOGANY SETTEE. Style of Samuel McIntire, carver, and Nehemiah Adams, frame-maker.
Salem, Mass., circa 1810

964. A VIRGINIA-WALNUT DROP-LEAF TABLE.
Pennsylvania, Early XVIII Century
J. Stogdell Stokes Collection.
Photograph by Taylor & Dull

965. A WALNUT DROP-LEAF TABLE.

AMERICAN FURNITURE

967. A Maple Butterfly Trestle Table.
New England, XVIII Century

966. A Virginia-Walnut Side Table.
Pennsylvania, Early XVIII Century
J. Stogdell Stokes Collection.
Photograph by Taylor & Dull

968. A Curly Maple Porringer Table. The feet of Yorkshire type.
American, XVIII Century

970. A Walnut Tray-Top Table.
Pennsylvania, XVIII Century

969. A Mahogany Tray-Top Table.
New England, XVIII Century

971. A Mahogany Drop-Leaf Table. American, XVIII Century

AMERICAN FURNITURE

973. A Mahogany Tripod Table.
Pennsylvania, XVIII Century

974. A Mahogany Tripod Table.
Pennsylvania, XVIII Century

972. A Mahogany Tripod Candle Stand. A type occasionally found in English collections; rare in America. Probably Salem, circa 1785.
New England, XVIII Century

975. A Mahogany Tripod Table with Piecrust Top.   Philadelphia, XVIII Century
Courtesy of Joe Kindig, Jr. & Son, York, Pennsylvania

977. A Mahogany Tray-Top Table. Made by John Goddard in 1763.
Newport, R. I., XVIII Century

976. A MAHOGANY TRIPOD TABLE WITH
PIECRUST TOP. Philadelphia, XVIII Century
Courtesy of Joe Kindig, Jr. & Son, York, Pennsylvania

978. A MAHOGANY TRAY-TOP TABLE. Style of John Goddard.
Newport, R. I., XVIII Century
Norvin H. Green Collection.
Photograph by Taylor & Dull

980. A MAHOGANY CARD TABLE. The knees carved with a version of the Irish leaf-clasp.
New York, XVIII Century
Norvin H. Green Collection.
Photograph by Taylor & Dull

979. A MAHOGANY DROP-LEAF TABLE. Probably New York; some necessary restoration.
American, XVIII Century
Norvin H. Green Collection.
Photograph by Taylor & Dull

AMERICAN FURNITURE

981. A MAHOGANY CARD TABLE. Style of John Goddard. Newport, R. I., XVIII Century

982. A MAHOGANY CARD TABLE. With apron centering the "Philadelphia peanut," a widely used form of cabochon ornament.
Philadelphia, XVIII Century
Norvin H. Green Collection.
Photograph by Taylor & Dull

A DIRECTORY OF ANTIQUE FURNITURE

983. A Chippendale Mahogany Drop-Leaf Table. With Marlborough legs as employed in England and Ireland, appearing in early nineteenth century cost lists as "Marlbro' legs."
American, XVIII Century

985. A Chippendale Mahogany Side Table. From a Baltimore collection.
American, XVIII Century

984. A Chippendale Walnut and Mahogany Side Table. Formerly owned by Stephen Van Rensselaer.
American, XVIII Century

AMERICAN FURNITURE

986. A Hepplewhite Mahogany Pembroke Table.
American, XVIII Century

987. A Hepplewhite Mahogany Pembroke Table. Formerly in the Van Rensselaer family.
American, XVIII Century

988. A Hepplewhite Mahogany Pembroke Table.
American, XVIII Century
Marsden J. Perry Collection.
Photograph by Taylor & Dull

989. A Hepplewhite Mahogany Card Table. With label of John Townsend.
Newport, R. I., XVIII Century

312 A DIRECTORY OF ANTIQUE FURNITURE

990. A Hepplewhite Mahogany Card Table.
With label of Elbert Anderson.
New York City, XVIII Century
Norvin H. Green Collection.
Photograph by Taylor & Dull

991. A Hepplewhite Mahogany Card Table.
John Hewitt, New York City, circa 1810

992. A Mahogany Card Table.
New England, circa 1800

993. A Mahogany Card Table.
New England, circa 1800

AMERICAN FURNITURE

995. A Sheraton Mahogany and Maple Occasional Table.
New England, circa 1800

996. A Sheraton Mahogany Sewing Table. American, circa 1810

994. A Sheraton Mahogany Tripod Candle Stand.
New England, circa 1810
Norvin H. Green Collection.
Photograph by Taylor & Dull

997. A Mahogany Work Table. The carving attributed to Samuel McIntire.
Salem, Mass., circa 1810

998. A Mahogany Cellaret. With label of Joseph Rawson and Son.
Providence, R. I., circa 1810

A DIRECTORY OF ANTIQUE FURNITURE

999. A Duncan Phyfe Mahogany Sewing Table.
New York City, circa 1810-1815

1000. A Sheraton Mahogany Pembroke Table.
American, circa 1810

1001. A Duncan Phyfe Mahogany Pembroke Table.
New York City, circa 1810-1815

AMERICAN FURNITURE

1002. A Duncan Phyfe Mahogany Drop-Leaf Table.
New York City, circa 1810-1820

1003. A Duncan Phyfe Mahogany Drop-Leaf Table.
New York City, circa 1810-1820

1004. A Mahogany Whatnot with Canterbury.
New York City, circa 1810
Ralph Blum Collection.
Photograph by Taylor & Dull

1005. A SHERATON MAHOGANY CARD TABLE.
New England, circa 1800

1006. A SHERATON MAHOGANY AND BIRD'S-EYE MAPLE CARD TABLE. Attributed to John Seymour and Son. Boston, circa 1805
Norvin H. Green Collection.
Photograph by Taylor & Dull

1008. A SHERATON MAHOGANY AND BRANCH SATINWOOD CARD TABLE.
Massachusetts, circa 1810
Andrew M. Williams Collection.
Photograph by Taylor & Dull

1007. A SHERATON MAHOGANY AND BRANCH SATINWOOD CARD TABLE.
Massachusetts, circa 1810

AMERICAN FURNITURE

1009. A Sheraton Mahogany Card Table.
New York City, circa 1810

1010. A Mahogany Folding Side Table. Resembling the work of George Woodruff.
New York City, circa 1810

1011. A Duncan Phyfe Mahogany Tripod Card Table.   New York City, circa 1810

1012. A Duncan Phyfe Mahogany Tripod Card Table.
New York City, circa 1810-1815

1013. A HEPPLEWHITE MAHOGANY MIXING BOARD. With inset marble top. New England, XVIII Century
Courtesy of Joe Kindig, Jr. & Son, York, Pennsylvania

1014. A HEPPLEWHITE MAHOGANY SIDEBOARD. New England, XVIII Century
Marsden J. Perry Collection.
Photograph by Taylor & Dull

AMERICAN FURNITURE

1015. A Hepplewhite Mahogany Sideboard.
American, XVIII Century

1016. A Hepplewhite Mahogany Sideboard. With label of
Elbert Anderson, Maiden Lane (1789-1796).
New York City, XVIII Century

Norvin H. Green Collection.
Photograph by Taylor & Dull

1017. A Hepplewhite Mahogany Sideboard.
New Jersey, XVIII Century

Ralph Blum Collection.
Photograph by Taylor & Dull

1018. A Hepplewhite Mahogany Sideboard.
Baltimore, Md., XVIII Century

AMERICAN FURNITURE 321

1019. A Sheraton Mahogany and Branch
Satinwood Sideboard.
Massachusetts, circa 1800

1021. A Mahogany Sideboard.
Salem, Mass., circa 1810

1020. A Sheraton Mahogany Sideboard.
Massachusetts, circa 1810

A DIRECTORY OF ANTIQUE FURNITURE

1023. A Duncan Phyfe Mahogany Dining Table.
New York City, circa 1810-1820

1022. A Duncan Phyfe Mahogany Dining Table.
New York City, circa 1810-1820

1024. A Duncan Phyfe Mahogany Dining Table.
New York City, circa 1810-1820

Norvin H. Green Collection.
Photograph by Taylor & Dull

1025. A Mahogany Dining Table. Resembling the work of Duncan Phyfe, but also that of other work currently produced.
New York City, circa 1810

AMERICAN FURNITURE

1026. A WALNUT LOWBOY.
New England, XVIII Century

1027. A WALNUT LOWBOY.
Philadelphia, XVIII Century

1028. A WALNUT LOWBOY.
Philadelphia, XVIII Century
Norvin H. Green Collection.
Photograph by Taylor & Dull

A DIRECTORY OF ANTIQUE FURNITURE

1029. A CHERRYWOOD LOWBOY. With tray top.
New England, XVIII Century
George M. Curtis Collection.
Photograph by Taylor & Dull

1030. A MAHOGANY LOWBOY.
Philadelphia, XVIII Century

1031. A WALNUT LOWBOY.
Philadelphia, XVIII Century

AMERICAN FURNITURE

1033. A MAHOGANY LOWBOY. The top apparently loosened and refitted, an injury sustained by many lowboys.
Philadelphia, XVIII Century
Marsden J. Perry Collection.
Photograph by Taylor & Dull

1032. A MAHOGANY LOWBOY. Recorded as originally owned by General Lewis Morris, Morristown, N. Y.
Philadelphia, XVIII Century

1034. A MAHOGANY LOWBOY. Matching the highboy shown in Fig. 1043; both carved beneath their inset colonettes with vertical leaf motifs.
Philadelphia, XVIII Century

A DIRECTORY OF ANTIQUE FURNITURE

1035. A WALNUT AND PINE CABINET-ON-STAND.
Massachusetts, Early XVIII Century

1036. A VIRGINIA WALNUT HIGHBOY. With some necessary restoration.
Pennsylvania, Early XVIII Century

AMERICAN FURNITURE 327

1037. A Maple Highboy.
New England, XVIII Century

1039. A Cherrywood Highboy.
New England, XVIII Century

1038. A Maple Highboy.
New England, XVIII Century
Ralph Blum Collection.
Photograph by Taylor & Dull.

1041. A WALNUT HIGHBOY. A fine example, harmed to some extent by loss of applied scrolls which flanked the two shells, replaced by incised scrolls. Philadelphia, XVIII Century

1040. A WALNUT HIGHBOY. New England, XVIII Century

1043. A MAHOGANY HIGHBOY. The vertical leaf motif above the four knees borrowed from Irish designs. Philadelphia, XVIII Century

1044. A Walnut Highboy.
Philadelphia, XVIII Century

1042. A Mahogany Highboy.
Philadelphia, XVIII Century

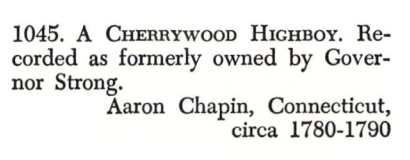

1045. A Cherrywood Highboy. Recorded as formerly owned by Governor Strong.
Aaron Chapin, Connecticut, circa 1780-1790

AMERICAN FURNITURE

1048. A Mahogany Tambour Writing Cabinet. Massachusetts, circa 1800

1047. A Mahogany Writing Cabinet. With label of Joseph Rawson and Son. Providence, R. I., circa 1800

A DIRECTORY OF ANTIQUE FURNITURE

1046. A MAHOGANY TAMBOUR WRITING DESK.
New England, circa 1800

1049. A MAHOGANY TAMBOUR WRITING
CABINET. Attributed to John Seymour and Son.
Boston, Mass., circa 1810
*Norvin H. Green Collection.
Photograph by Taylor & Dull*

1050. A MAHOGANY WRITING CABINET.
Massachusetts, circa 1820

AMERICAN FURNITURE

1051. A Carved Oak Hadley Chest.
Connecticut, Late XVII Century

1052. An Oak and Pine Press Cupboard.
New England, Late XVII Century

334 A DIRECTORY OF ANTIQUE FURNITURE

1054. A Painted and Decorated Dower Chest.
Pennsylvania, dated 1803

1055. A Maple Desk. The writing interior restored.
New England, XVIII Century

1053. A Painted and Decorated Dower Chest.
Pennsylvania, dated 1795

AMERICAN FURNITURE

1058. A Walnut Chest-on-Chest.
New England, XVIII Century

1057. A Maple Secretary. With inscription describing its execution in New Hampshire, in 1778.
New England, XVIII Century

1056. A Cherrywood Secretary.
New England, XVIII Century

A DIRECTORY OF ANTIQUE FURNITURE

1060. A Cherrywood Secretary. With label of Webb & Scott. Providence, R. I., circa 1800

1061. A Cherrywood Corner Cupboard. With interior shell niche. Pennsylvania, XVIII Century
Ralph Blum Collection.
Photograph by Taylor & Dull

1059. A Cherrywood Secretary. Aaron Chapin, Connecticut, circa 1785

AMERICAN FURNITURE

1063. A Mahogany Yoke-Front Desk.
New England, XVIII Century
Norvin H. Green Collection.
Photograph by Taylor & Dull

1064. A Mahogany Yoke-Front Desk.
New England, XVIII Century

1062. A Mahogany Yoke-Front Chest of Drawers. The form incorrectly termed "oxbow," or U-shaped.
New England, XVIII Century
Ralph Blum Collection.
Photograph by Taylor & Dull

338 A DIRECTORY OF ANTIQUE FURNITURE

1065. A MAHOGANY YOKE-FRONT SECRETARY.
New England, XVIII Century
Norvin H. Green Collection.
Photograph by Taylor & Dull

1066. A MAHOGANY AND CHERRYWOOD
YOKE-FRONT SECRETARY.
New England, XVIII Century

AMERICAN FURNITURE

1067. A GODDARD-TOWNSEND MAHOGANY BLOCK-FRONT KNEEHOLE COMMODE. The vogue of block-front furniture extended from c. 1765 to c. 1795.   Newport, R. I., circa 1800
George M. Curtis Collection.
Photograph by Taylor & Dull

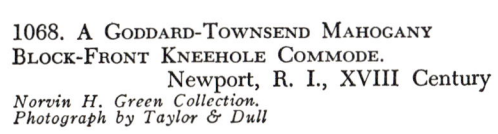

1068. A GODDARD-TOWNSEND MAHOGANY BLOCK-FRONT KNEEHOLE COMMODE.
Newport, R. I., XVIII Century
Norvin H. Green Collection.
Photograph by Taylor & Dull

1069. A Cherrywood Block-Front Chest of Drawers. Connecticut, XVIII Century

1070. A Mahogany Block-Front Kneehole Commode. New York, XVIII Century

1071. A Mahogany Block-Front Chest of Drawers. Discovered in a London Museum devoted to the study of English cabinetwork. New England, XVIII Century
Courtesy of the Geffrye Museum, London

AMERICAN FURNITURE

1073. A Mahogany Block-Front Desk.
New England, XVIII Century

1072. A Mahogany Block-Front Desk.
New England, XVIII Century

1074. A Mahogany Block-Front Desk. Recorded as made by John Goddard and as having descended in the Townsend family.
New England, XVIII Century

1077. A Mahogany Block-Front Secretary. Lip-molded drawers are seldom found in Newport block-front pieces, except those made by Job Townsend. The usual plainly finished drawer front, with cockbead planted on the surrounding surfaces, is associated with Continental work more than with English practice. New England, XVIII Century
Norvin H. Green Collection.
Photograph by Taylor & Dull

1076. A Mahogany Block-Front Secretary. New England, XVIII Century

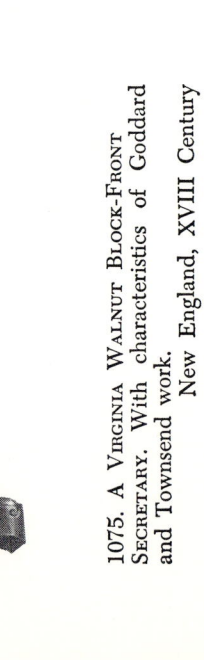

1075. A Virginia Walnut Block-Front Secretary. With characteristics of Goddard and Townsend work. New England, XVIII Century

AMERICAN FURNITURE

1078. A Mahogany Kettle-Base Secretary. According to tradition this piece was obtained from Sir William Pepperell between 1790 and 1800, while he was residing in Portsmouth, N. H. Sir William, grandson of the famous hero of Louisburg, was a Royalist who departed from these shores in 1775, being proscribed in 1778, when his estate was confiscated and sold. Massachusetts, XVIII Century
Ralph Blum Collection.
Photograph by Taylor & Dull

1079. A Mahogany Chest-on-Chest. A piece which had previously changed hands at a very low figure. Recognition of structural features which associated it with the preceding secretary placed it in an entirely different price bracket. Massachusetts, XVIII Century
Ralph Blum Collection.
Photograph by Taylor & Dull

1080. A Mahogany Chest-on-Chest
Philadelphia, XVIII Century

AMERICAN FURNITURE

1081. A Mahogany Desk.
New York, XVIII Century

1082. A Mahogany Chest-on-Chest.
New York, XVIII Century

1084. A Mahogany Serpentine-Front Chest of Drawers. From Camden, Maine.
American, XVIII Century

1083. A Mahogany Writing Cabinet. Apparently a New York City piece. American, XVIII Century

1085. A Mahogany Bow-Front Chest of Drawers. American, XVIII Century

AMERICAN FURNITURE

1087. A MAHOGANY CHEST OF DRAWERS. With deeply swept serpentine front; the top edge inlaid with a triple banding, a favored treatment in Baltimore and in Dublin.
American, XVIII Century

1086. A HEPPLEWHITE MAHOGANY COMMODE. Salem, Mass., XVIII Century

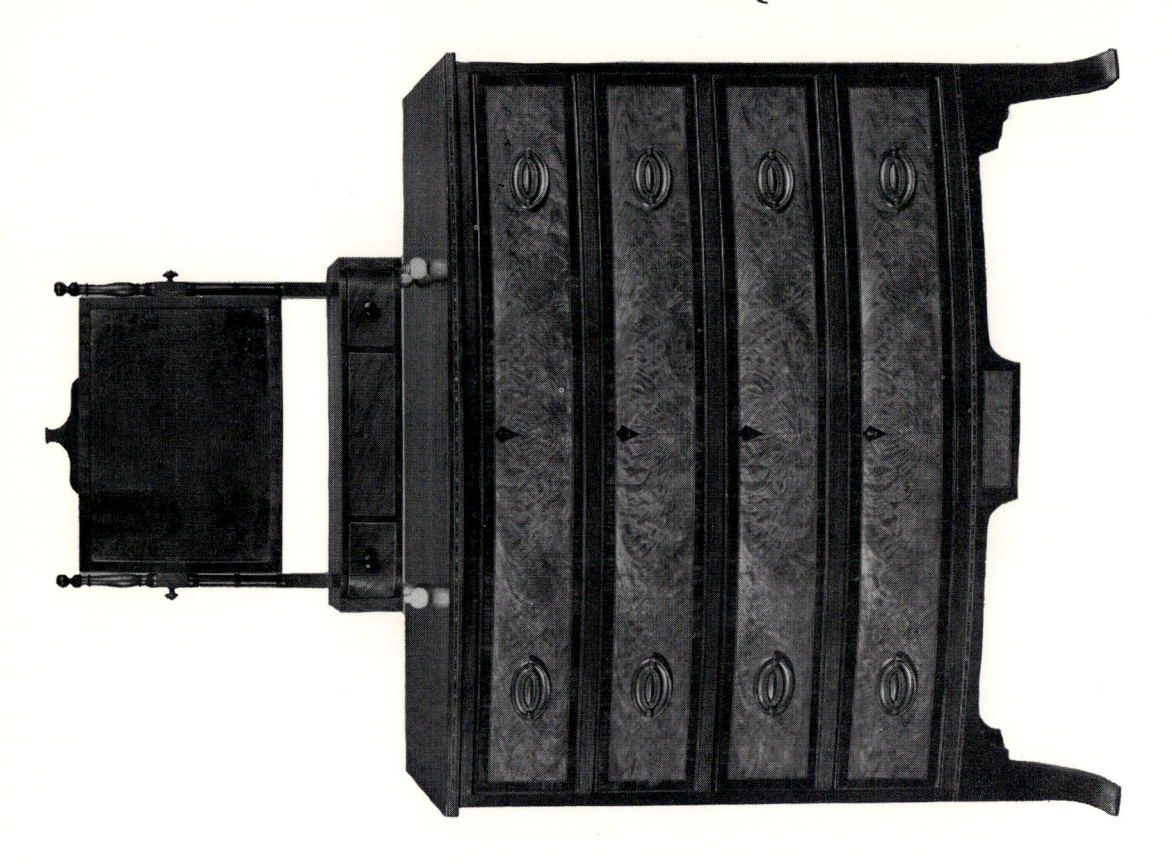

1088. A Mahogany and Branch Satinwood Chest of Drawers. New England, circa 1800
*Andrew M. Williams Collection.
Photograph by Taylor & Dull*

1089. A Cherrywood Desk. New Berlin, N. Y., circa 1810-1820

1091. A Mahogany and Branch Satinwood Cabinet. American, circa 1800

1090. A Mahogany Tambour Writing Cabinet. New England, circa 1800

1092. A Mahogany Secretary-Cabinet. The general design characteristic of Salem craftsmen such as Nehemiah Adams.
New England, circa 1800

AMERICAN FURNITURE

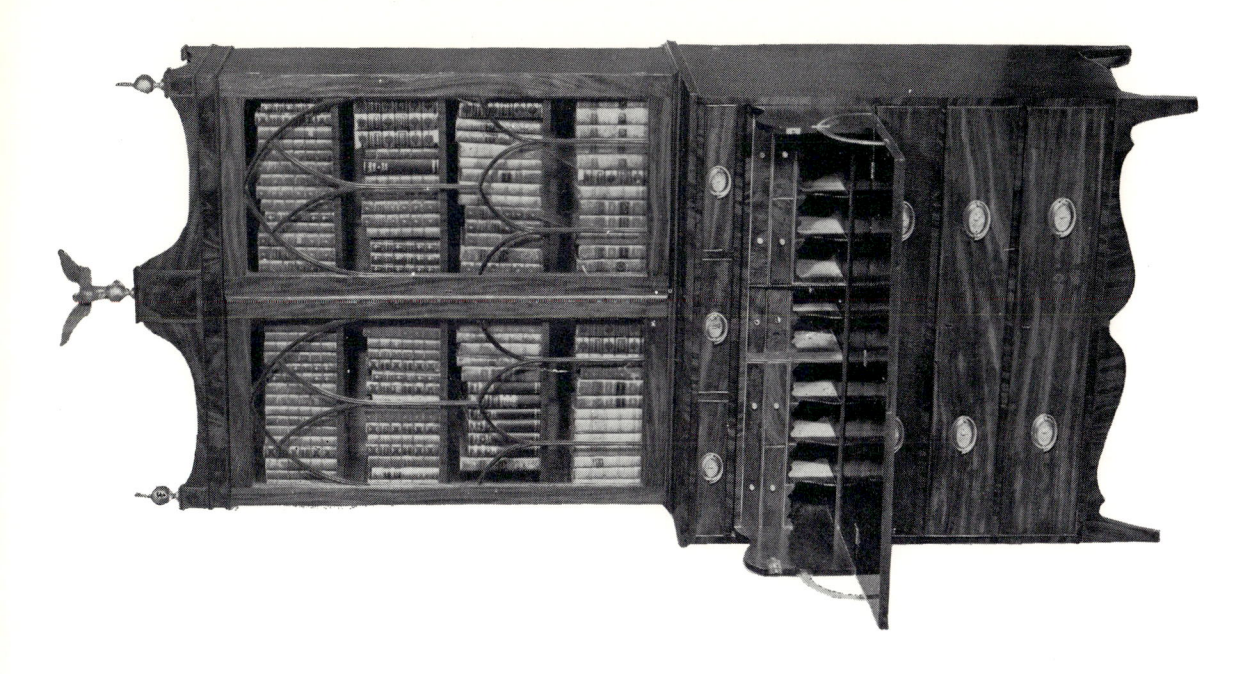

1094. A Mahogany Secretary. From Geneva, N. Y. American, circa 1810

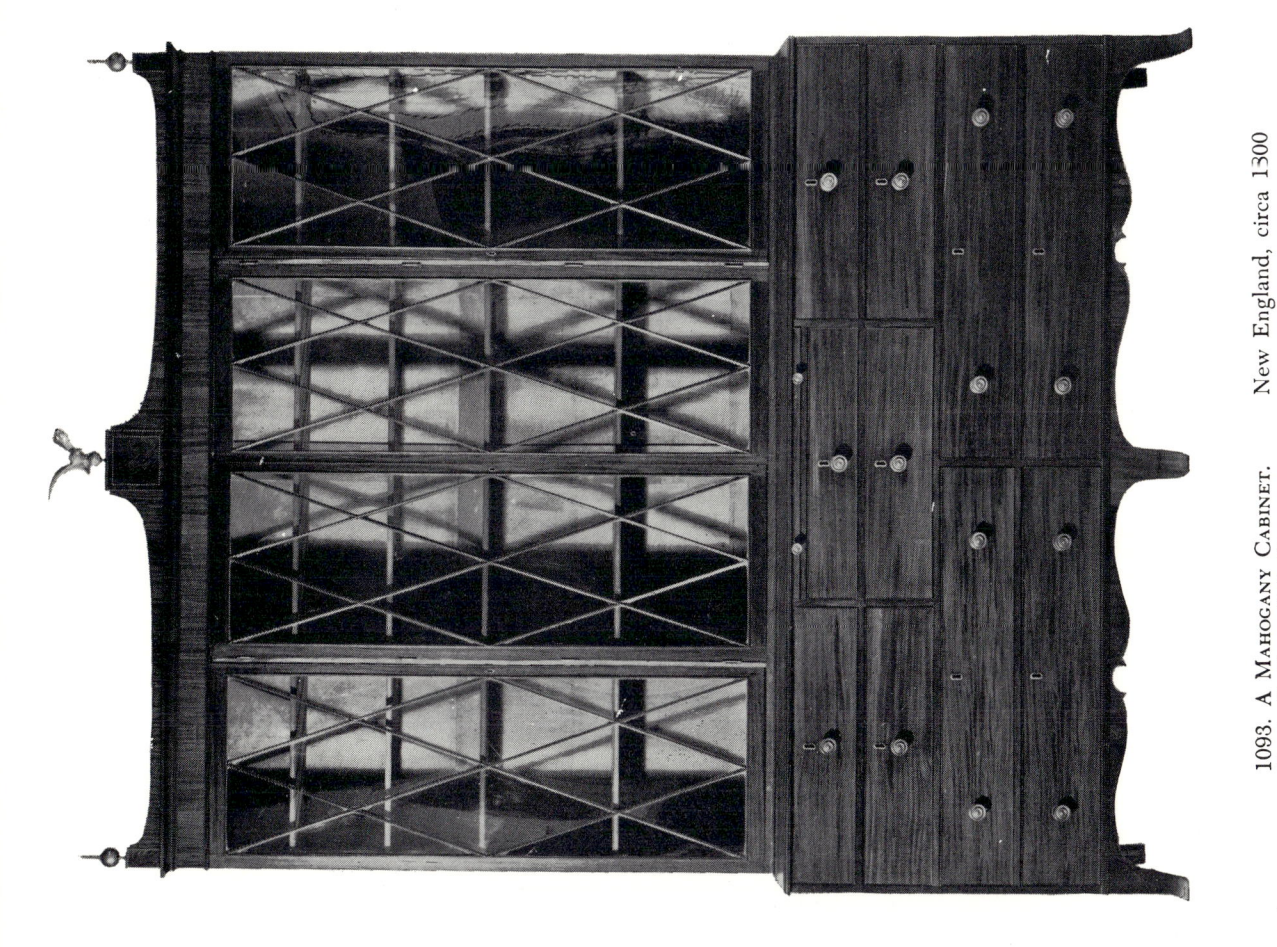

1093. A Mahogany Cabinet. New England, circa 1800
*Norvin H. Green Collection.
Photograph by Taylor & Dull*

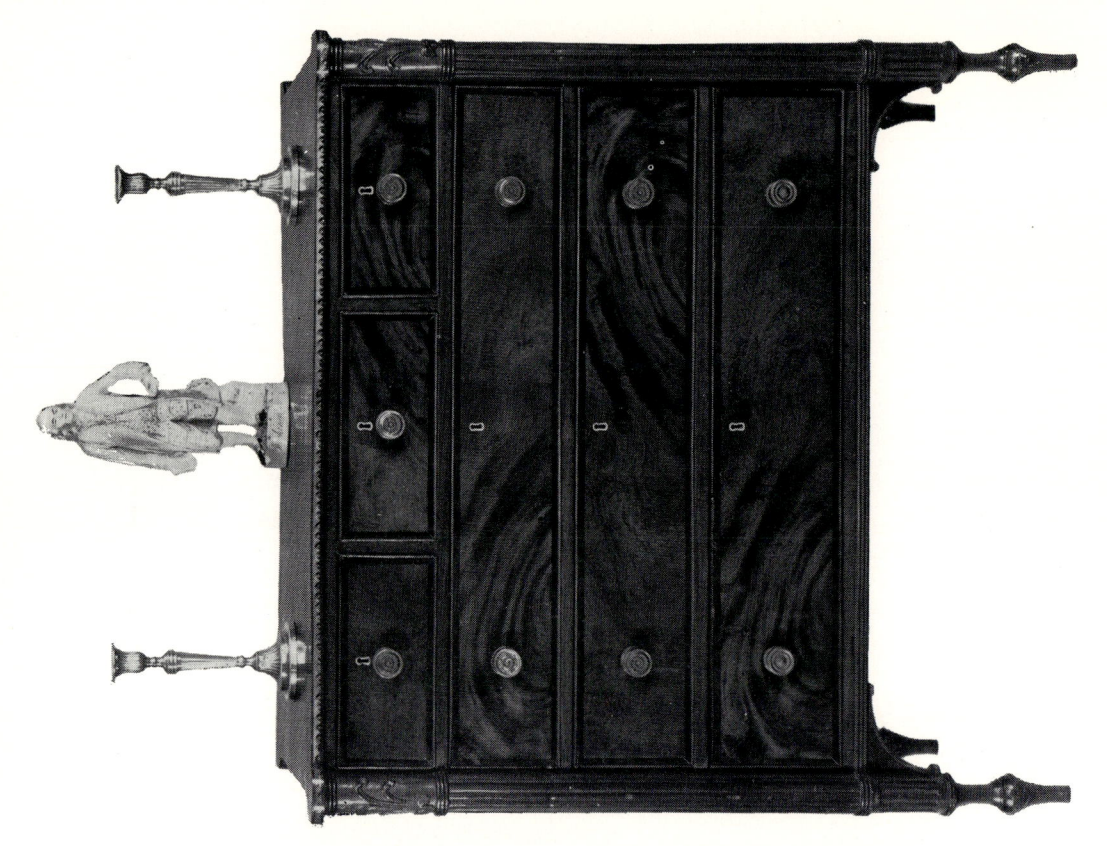

1096. A Mahogany Chest of Drawers. Massachusetts, circa 1810

1095. A Mahogany Chest of Drawers. Salem, Mass., circa 1810

AMERICAN FURNITURE

1098. A Mahogany Cylinder-Front Writing Cabinet
New York, circa 1820

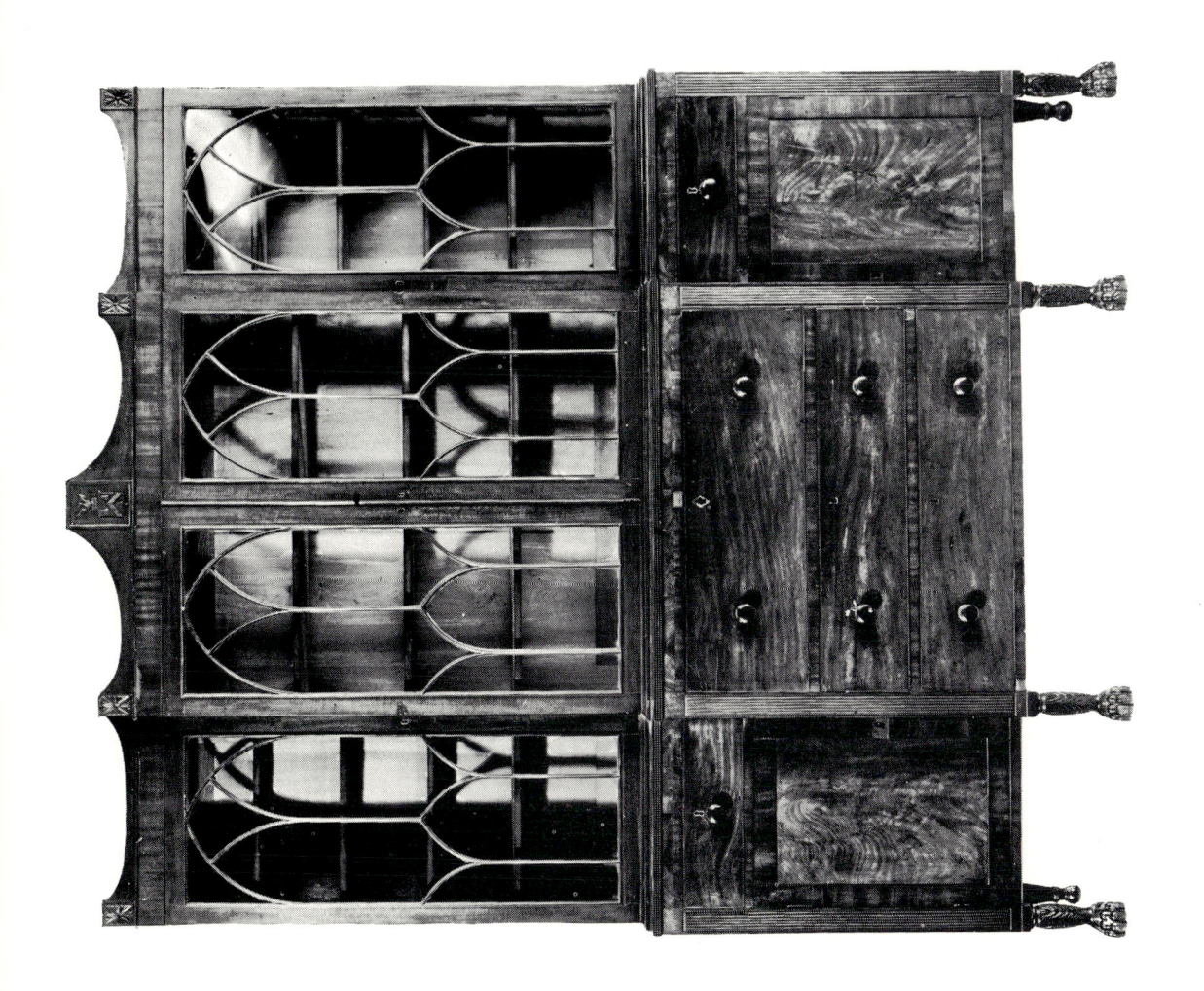

1097. A Mahogany Breakfront Cabinet.
With pediment centering the Chrystie coat of arms.
New York, circa 1820
*William Few Chrystie Collection.
Photograph by Taylor & Dull*

1100. A Gilded Wall Mirror. With commemorative panel centering an engraved portrait of George Washington. Label of James Stokes. Philadelphia, circa 1800
*Andrew M. Williams Collection.
Photograph by Taylor & Dull*

1102. A Mahogany Wall Mirror. With store label of John Elliott. American, circa 1805

1103. A Mahogany Wall Mirror. With label of Joseph and John Del Vecchio. Albany, N. Y., circa 1805
*Norvin H. Green Collection.
Photograph by Taylor & Dull*

AMERICAN FURNITURE

1099. A Gilded Wall Mirror. With *eglomisé* frieze panel centering an engraved portrait of George Washington, after a painting by William Savage. From the Van Rensselaer family. American, circa 1800

1101. A Gilded Pier Mirror with Eglomisé Panels. Boston or New York, circa 1805
Courtesy of Joe Kindig, Jr. & Son, York, Pennsylvania